SECOND LIFE® IS A PLACE WE VISIT

Second Life® is a place we visit

Collected articles on the metaverse

Huckleberry Hax

Contents

Preface

Hello Resident of Second Life. You are a resident of Second Life, I take it? Perhaps you're not and you're reading this because it's The Future and you'd like to know a little bit more about this virtual world craze that's recently taken off. Perhaps your son/daughter/spouse/partner/best friend now spends every second of their free time with an Oculus Rift headset strapped to their face – you have to synchronise putting pieces of food into their mouth with the rising of their virtual fork in the metaverse – and want to understand how in God's name this madness could possibly have happened. Well good for you. You have my permission to treat this book as cultural artefact. It won't tell you much about whatever virtual reality thing is popular right now, but it will tell you about some of the antics and issues which pervaded the pioneering days – for that is how we most assuredly will refer to them in retrospect – of Second Life, for Second Life (or 'SL', as we residents like to call it) is where virtual living began.

Or perhaps it's the future and you *were* a resident, once upon a time. SL is now a distant memory and you can hardly believe that you used to get so excited over such things as flexi-prims and dance club sploders. Good for you also. You have my permission to treat this book as a nostalgic walk down Memory Lane. Just don't forget in your rose-tinted recollections that those good old days were also responsible for the invention of the word 'freenis'.

Of course, you might be someone from the *far* future, sifting through the scraps which remain of early 21st century attempts to create virtual habitation, smiling sadly at the utter naivety of it all and how history never learned from the mistakes that were made in the intellectual ownership of inventory and the ghettoisation of adult playgrounds. Good for you as well. You have my permission to cite me as a reference in your thesis. I'm delighted that my book has made it to your time and hope you can forgive my generation for the whole ice caps thing.

But you might just still be an SL resident, a player in the great game (that's not a game) we currently call the metaverse, wanting to know other takes on our world or simply needing some writing about Second Life to fuel your addiction when you're on the train to work and can't actually be there. Good for you. You have my permission to treat this book as the e-cigarette to your metaphorical metaverse smoking habit. Unfortunately, this paragraph will go out of date a lot more quickly than the preceding ones.

What you hold in your hands is a collection of articles I've written over the last eight years on various aspects of SL (actually, it's much more like four years: I've artificially expanded the range by including an article from 2007 that was my only attempt at writing SL non-fiction until 2011; but you have to admit eight years makes me sound so much more learned). Some are irreverent banter. Some are attempts at being serious. Here and there, you'll find unashamed plugs for my novels (though since my novels are most of them set in SL or a similar sort of thing, I tell myself that this is all morally fine).

I should probably say something meaningful here about Second Life to get you in the mood for all the chapters to come. It's a funny old place. I still haven't quite got my head around it. I've seen the arrival of voice in my time (which never really took on), of sculpties (which were amazing, right up to the era of mesh, at which point they became about as desirable as dog turds), of windlight (which still stuns me), of shadows (just gorgeous) and of mesh (wow); I've seen SL rebranded as a business platform, an education platform, a 'creative space' and now a kickass virtual world, Rift-ready for the VR craze to come.

None of these marketings really quite captures it for me. I've seen places within SL come and go, I've seen groups come and go, I've seen people come and go, I've seen builds and events appear and then depart. It is a constantly changing metaverse and my thoughts about it constantly change also.

I don't think it's a second *life*, though. Whilst I might well hold a different opinion on the matter this time tomorrow, I more and more find my thoughts converging on the idea that SL is a place – one we visit for all manner of different reasons. Sometimes, the bleeding obvious needs to find its way into intellectual debate: we only actually have one life.

But enough of my attempting to solicit involuntary head nodding by sneaking in a superficially profound statement under the radar of irreverent banter. You have 42 chapters to read. Get going.

The language of love; the love of language: is SL about to lose the thing that makes it special?

First published May 2007, The Spork magazine

Sometimes I stand on the balcony at *Sumos Playpen* just to absorb the muddy mix of word play coming from the pit below. Newbies discovering the workings of their digital genitalia is rarely an aesthetically pleasing thing to behold - in either the visual or the aural sense - but just occasionally something from the soup of words flowing over the monitor is unique enough to catch my attention. The chatter between visiting mistresses and their slaves, for example, can have a slightly cheeky flavour to it that's a little more sophisticated than your average no-idea-what-to-say-but-I-think-it-should-contain-words-like-'throbbing' variety of comments. It's certainly better than the inane ramblings of Xcite! machinery and its 'earth shattering orgasms'; the less said about those the better. And between that and the prospect of live speech, which I understand looms ever closer to the mainstream SL experience, the water is clear and wide and blue.

When I look at the screen in SL now I see words living, bouncing around right there in front of me. At its worst it's just banter, and I guess there's nothing wrong with that (although, let's face it, it can get pretty bad at times); but at its best it's nothing short of poetry: a frame of mind, a sensation, an emotional state squeezed into a line of text that gives you goose bumps when you read it. Once I heard, "Feeling you wiping away my tears" from one of a couple holding each other at Sinners' Paradise, and it made the hairs on the back of my neck stand up.

What is it about text as our main means of communication in SL that brings out the poets in us? For sure it's rarely easy, and certainly I've failed to capture a feeling or something I wanted to say far more times than I've succeeded. I can't be the only one to have stared at a line of text and agonised over what should be my response... and ended up seeing the moment pass me by completely. Yet, for all my illiterate fumblings, the romance of the well-written word still captivates me, and I continue to relish the few extra moments of thought it affords me over speech, even when they end up amounting to nothing.

We pad out our speech with such guff sometimes. The errs and the umms are perhaps the tamest examples, where at least we're having the decency to communicate we're not quite sure what to say. Verbal communication comes just as naturally to us as walking, and therein lies the rub: whilst walking might be something we do without effort, that doesn't mean to say we're all walking as well as we could be. In speech, as with walking, we're all too accustomed to slouching when we know we should be thinking about our posture. Writing something down requires just that little bit more effort, and if we direct that effort correctly the results can be spectacular.

And what is it about text as our main means of communication in SL that can bring about such relish and delight over a few words read... or such worry and anxiety? Is it simply that we know instinctively that a comment written down is often meant more than one spoken? In speech we can embark upon a comment, think again, and divert it into something benign or non-committal before we're even half-way to the full-stop; or sometimes we don't and end up saying something we just don't mean at all. In text, however, we have until the last letter's written and the enter key pressed to change our mind, delete the whole lot, and say something else or settle for nothing at all. Is this why some residents seem compelled to express such intense devotion to their loved ones in their profiles? In our SL relationships, can we come to feel more loved and wanted than in our RL relationships, simply because we feel that someone committing words of love to writing implies more genuine affection than a glib, off-the-cuff comment (possibly said with attention on the television, possibly regretted by the speaker before they've even finished speaking it)? It's not just words of love, either; the merest of compliments offered by a new friend known for the shortest of moments can still cause me to sit up a little in my chair (find a person tomorrow and pay them a beautiful compliment - and mean it - and watch how they become bigger in front of you). These are the words I relish most of all, and often I gaze upon them the full fifteen default seconds that they sit at the bottom of my screen before finally dissolving away.

What will become of places such as Sumos Playpen when voice communication becomes the norm in SL? Will a balcony viewpoint of the future treat the observer to a gurgle of gasps and grunting noises from all around the world? Will the triumph of technology be to deliver the sounds of 20 different people achieving solo climax with their virtual partners? Oh... The... Horror...

And what will become of sunset conversations at Sinners' Paradise, of excited greetings and lingering farewells, of pain and sadness held tight by those who care, of contrition, of forgiveness, of simple compliments and thankyous that hang in the air like perfume? Will the so-called technological breakthrough of speech become the end of a brief, but golden resurgence of the written word's ability to reach deep and touch us? If I was playing an on-line game and needed my fingers free to control my weaponry then voice communication would probably be a blessing indeed, but SL is all about relationships and, for me, text is the thing that makes those special.

2

Happy Birthday Second Life

First published June 2011, huckleberryhax.blogspot.com

The significance of SL's eighth birthday must surely be that we're now closer to the tenth birthday than the fifth. Last year, it would have been reasonable to look at the 'value added,' two years on from five, rather than get distracted too much by the monolith that is ten lurking on the other side of the visible horizon. But, with the passing of 'eight years old,' ten is now in sight and we can avert our gaze no longer. True, we might need a sturdy set of binoculars to spot it at this distance, but it's unmistakably there – a tiny little blob on the skyline, waiting for us with its smug arms folded and a fat cigar wedged between its grinning teeth.

Is there any point in speculating on the question, 'What will SL be like in two years' time?' Probably not. Personally, I think it likely it won't be a great deal different than it is today. This is not to detract from such developments as mesh, depth of field and shadows – and whatever two or three new enhancements are delivered by then (I'm counting on avatar physics being extended to male genitalia, myself) – these are all well and good, and I'm sure we'll all have much fun ignoring them completely whilst we continue to crucify Linden for its viewer strategy. But will my hours per evening spent in front of the computer feel qualitatively different then from the hours I spent back in 2007? I doubt it very much. If graphical complexity mattered that much to me, I'd have thrown my sculpted prim oar in years ago and gone and bought myself an X-Box.

Not that I'm saying it doesn't matter, of course. It matters a great deal, particularly to many of the newcomers to SL, who imagine it to be, I suppose, the peacetime equivalent of Call of Duty; a world where the dust of virtual warfare might well be settled, but you could still write your name in it with your finger if you chose to do so. The fact that every last texture in SL has to be downloaded from a distant server, rather than springing majestically into high definition action from the nearby cosiness of a hard drive, tends rather to be lost on gaming veterans and offers little compensation for the wheezy, delayed arrival of a brick texture that was not only late but had to sit down for a rest and a restorative cup of tea when it got here. And therein lies the problem: no advances in mesh or lighting or bouncy body parts can possibly lure to our world any person expecting the full-on graphic immediacy of modern 3D gaming. It's not Linden's fault that internet and server speeds aren't yet up to the standard required of such an experience, but this truth will be neither apparent nor of interest to the newcomer who drops by one day because they've "always been meaning to find out what this Second Life thing is all about" and ends up concluding that it "doesn't seem to work very well."

Because the thing that would *actually* make SL feel different would be if more people were using it. By which I mean enough people that the words 'second life' no longer carry with them that conditioned response involving a badly concealed smirk and an almost irrepressible desire on my part to use the physical intervention of my fist with which to effect its removal. Accompanied, I hasten to add, by the slightly hysterically shrieked question, "If your real life is so fucking wonderful, why exactly do you piss away so much of it in front of the TV?" That's what *really* irritates me. If Barack Obama wanted to dress me down for a life less meaningfully lived then that would be fair play, but how exactly is a TV diet of 'Ugly Betty,' 'X Factor' and Channel Four's 'Embarrassing bodies' a safe platform from which to launch judgements upon the quality of my social interactions?

These, then, are the two elements of SL which probably won't have changed by June 2013: the non-users' bafflement over its appeal and our own general reluctance to defend it in any manner that roughly approximates 'assertive'. Whatever new embellishments come along between now and then, life inworld for most of us will be as much the guilty pleasure of a secret cigarette as it was when we first looked past the technological limitations and realised there was something to this virtual world. The visible hooks just aren't apparent to the rest of the human population: they weren't then; they're not now and they won't be in two years time. *Unless...*

Unless something unexpected happens. Because unexpected developments are how internet evolution occurs. These random mutations, these out-of-the-blue fluctuations in mainstream attentiveness are the stumbling, slightly drunken footsteps that have come to characterise the online 'march' of progress. If the right match is struck in the right place at the right time; if the right SL *something* manages to catch the interest of the general public, *then* it'll suddenly be big. It could be a YouTube video that just happens to use metaverse graphics. It could be a song that just happens to be about virtual relationships. It could be a novel that just happens to be set in SL.

Let's suppose its the latter. In fact, let's suppose it's one of *my* novels. Here's my plan: if you want SL to make it big in the future – and you *do* want SL to make it big in the future, don't you? - do your bit and buy my novels today. More importantly, buy extra copies to give to all your friends, not forgetting to prefix the giving of these generous gifts with the phrase, "I thought you might like a copy of that book that everyone's been talking about."

You're welcome, Second Life. Many Happy Returns.

3

Free Lindens? Thanks, but no thanks

First published August 2011, huckleberryhax.blogspot.com

A visit to a charming beach resort recently saw a mildly unpleasant exchange with the owner when his somethingorother script thing offered my companion free money. It was one of those random money givers you used to get all the time in *the good old days* of SL, when you weren't really living if your senses weren't being assailed by tat of some description on a minute-by-minute basis. And the amount was three Lindens.

By my calculation, three Lindens equals approximately just over one American cent. Not even a single British penny. Let me ask you something: if a complete stranger in real life walked up to you and pressed *one cent* into your hands, what exactly would your reaction be?

Of course, this is Second Life – not real life – and a penny buys you more in the virtual world than it does in the big outside. Why, a pair of jeans, for example, can be easily had for just two hundred Lindens – let's say the sort of jeans that might cost you $20 in real life. In this case, the 'real value' of our three Lindens rises to a staggering thirty cents! Still not very convincing in the stranger scenario, though, is it?

Oh yes, in the days when we were new and still sticking to that I'm-not-going-to-spend-any-money-on-Second-Life rule; in the days when we were willing to mop floors or clean windows or do whatever other pretend task was required of camp spots (because we had no virtual friends back then to feel humiliated in front of); in the days when all we wanted was to buy a hair style that didn't look like something had melted all over our heads then we took our two or three Lindens for the half hour of our time and we were thankful.

But then we discovered dignity. We decided it wasn't okay for our time to be owned so indifferently, and for such a pitifully small amount of money. In any case, by that time we'd pretty much become addicted to SL and found the funds to improve our inworld appearance elsewhere, like by cancelling our gym membership or through buying less vegetables.

Camp spots, of course, were – still are, in a few persistent cases – all about attracting people to a place. The more paid avatars you could have in your venue – so the logic went – the more popular it would appear and the more people might come check it out and maybe spend some *real* money. In return for a trifling expenditure, you got those valuable green dots on the map and a higher ranking in search. It didn't work as a strategy because most arrivals – on seeing that a place was only filled with campers – turned around and went back the way they came. Which brings us to the random money giver: same outlay, same penny-chasing newbies, same all-important little green dots, but no camping spots whatsoever to cause us veteran SL snobs to turn up our noses and leave.

Do I have a thing about random money givers? Not really. I'm pretty much neutral on the random money giver issue. I think it likely that orientation to this topic will be entirely dependent on who you are in SL and what sort of experience you've had therein. To the newbie chasing that hairstyle, it might indeed be glorious generosity. To an old hack like me, however, I can't deny that whiff, that hint, that soupçon of resentment aroused by the suspicion that someone might think I chose to visit a place just for the prospect of a measly couple of Lindens.

As for my innocent companion, she hadn't encountered random money givers before, was confused as to why it had been offered and promptly returned it to the person she was told had paid it. Amongst the comments subsequently made to me by the owner was that he'd never before encountered someone with such an "attitude problem" towards receiving free money: he was actually *angry* that his tiny gift had been turned down. He even threatened to ban us.

Is it *really* so unusual, so extraordinary an occurrence that someone might not consider 'free money' a significant improvement on their day? Is it *really* the supposition held by society that no gift of cash - no matter how small the amount, no matter how unknown the source is – should ever be turned down or questioned? In my flesh and blood life, I've turned down free things on many an occasion, as it happens. When UK supermarket Tesco briefly offered free tins of beans to its customers, for example, I didn't rush to the stores. It wasn't that I don't like beans or was suspicious of this strategy, it was simply that I didn't want to be part of a crowd who would drop everything for the sake of a few free tins of food which I didn't in any case need (I was perfectly happy with the idea that people for whom this would make a significant financial difference could stock up on the stuff unhindered by the likes of me, for whom it wouldn't). Did Tesco write to me demanding to know why their loyalty card database indicated I had not taken advantage of their generosity? They did not.

It was a bizarre few minutes of interaction at the beach: for all the immense work that had gone into creating a truly beautiful sim, the owner was prepared to eject precisely the sort of customer he wanted to attract just because they declined to accept his free tin of beans. It was a reminder that business and a short temper don't go well together, and that SL is truly an odd place to be sometimes. Also, however, it was funny. As anecdote material, it's added to that sense of actually having been somewhere – like the memory of the grumpy hotelier who moaned when you checked in late and requested a sandwich five minutes before the restaurant was due to close – and increased the sense of immersion, the fairy dust that makes SL real.

It occurs to me that there's the remote possibility this was actually his intent. If this is the case then I retract everything I've said above: you, sir, are a genius.

4

On bullying, griefing and performance art

First published August 2011, nordanomjorden.wordpress.com

Ah, Second Life: the place where colour means nothing. The place where status means nothing. The place where gender identity and sexuality mean nothing – nothing at all! The place where people can just get along. I suspect you can see where this one's going. Generally speaking, the understanding of the immense possibility offered by Second Life for human interaction comes along – if at all – after the realisation that it's yet another place for people to behave like dicks in. It's no different from any other place on the planet. Well, why should it be?

In fact, it's worse. Anonymity plays a key role in this, which is topical, given the recent hoo-haa concerning the banning of Google+ accounts where false names are used. I happen to be strongly in favour of pseudonyms on the internet (all the reasons for which can be found at http://my.nameis.me), but the price we pay for this is the occasional abuse of that extra layer of separation between behaviour and consequence. Anyone who has reason to moderate their behaviour in the real world (that pretty much includes all of us) can find on the internet the freedom to step outside of this 'constraint' if they choose to do so. One of the prices of anonymity is bullying.

Although it's not quite anonymity, is it? Calling it that, in fact, rather misses one of the most important points about bullying, which is that it almost always requires an audience of some description. The bully wants to be seen because the bully wants to impress. The bully does actually want people to say, "That's the work of so-and-so. Aren't they impressive?" A truly anonymous action would involve something done by someone no-one had ever heard of before, and with no secret clues so that the intended audience could nudge and wink at the tell-tale footprints. It occurs to me that what most people think of as individual griefing – the newbie at an info-hub who walks around naked and tells everyone to get a life, for example – is anonymous in this respect; bullying isn't. Bullying and griefing in SL, then, are distinct: griefing is targeted at wide groups of people who usually have no idea who the griefer is; bullying, on the other hand, is targeted at specific individuals, and victims and audience alike know exactly who the perpetrator is (though not enough for there to be any real life consequences). Both are forms of abuse, but griefing is far more easily endured, since victims are rarely alone in their experience. Griefing is not so personal.

I've recently had reason to think quite a bit about bullying in SL, not least because I fell susceptible myself to one of the rationalisation traps that can actually perpetuate bullying behaviour. More about that later. My RL occupation brings me into regular contact with schools and colleges, in which – so the media would have us believe – bullying is born and bred. (It isn't, by the way: the capacity to bully is something we're all created with and schools are just the first social context we encounter where it can serve a purpose. Genetically, it stems from the period when we lived in tribes and our safety depended on belonging: making someone else the target for ridicule makes it less likely we'll be picked on ourselves. And belonging, incidentally, is not the same as being liked, which has been known for decades: Maslow's famous 'hierarchy of need,' for example, places the need to belong below the need to be liked and above the need for security; bullies, then – contrary to the popular adage – don't necessarily 'just want to be liked'). The vast majority of bullying in schools – about 80% of it – is still non-electronic. The intense interest in cyber-bullying, then, comes not from its overall frequency, but from the fact that its impact has been found by research to be more damaging than 'conventional' bullying.

Why might this be? In the first place, the audience is larger. Rather than just being restricted to a locally known group of people, online bullying is witnessed potentially by an international audience. It opens up the possibility that new, previously unknown people, can join in with the pointing and the jeering, and that comments made by them can feed back on and influence the people that we do know. Second, there is no escape. No longer can we get away from bullying simply by going home and no longer is there is there any time of day in which bullying can't occur. Third, electronic media makes it more easy to distribute highly personal details about a victim, such as the contents of a private conversation or a humiliating image or video. Fourth, the issue of anonymity from sanctions. The intended audience might know who 'Bronson_889' is, but there's no official link to the guy who lives at number 53 without some serious police work.

What, then, constitutes cyber-bullying? A recent definition gives it as this: "electronically mediated behaviours among peers such as making fun of, telling lies, spreading rumours, threats and sharing private information or pictures without permission to do so." In the case of SL, peers can be taken to mean community members, whatever particular community that may be. There are of course thousands of them, but I'm going to concentrate here on the art community and for two reasons. First of all, it's where I've most recently witnessed cyber-bullying, but the main reason is that there appears to be a belief amongst some art community members that this sort of behaviour doesn't actually constitute bullying at all, but instead some sort of clever artistic expression.

Turning up at and disrupting someone's art event, they say, isn't bullying, it's protest against 'bad art' – it's 'livening up a dull event,' in fact. Targeting insults towards people in public chat, they say – isn't bullying, it's clever wit (we're not talking about comedy genius here, by the way, but comments that struggle to achieve even the sophistication of teenage jeers, like, "you're so boring.") Repeatedly hitting someone in front of others with a stick and following them wherever they go isn't bullying. Publishing private IMs on a public blog isn't bullying. It's art. It's all just art.

Art – in my opinion – is more a subjective experience than an objective one. Aesthetic pleasure varies from person to person, depending on their preferences and perception, and its experience may indeed be encountered in scenes that others find distasteful. But experiencing something as artistic does not make it not bullying. And it is not a justification for that act.

What was the trap I fell into? For all the insights into bullying I thought I had, I fell for the old 'he/she invites the bullying' rationalization. The problem with anti-bullying campaigns (see, for example, the 'Let's beat it together' cyber-bullying video on YouTube) is that they often present bully victims as perfect people that it's impossible to imagine did anything to merit them becoming a target. The reality is far messier than that. Bully victims don't necessarily just take their victimisation quietly. They sometimes lash back. They sometimes kick and punch. They sometimes scream in frustration. Sometimes, it is the expression of a personal belief or the absence of a social skill that leads to people being targeted, but the expression of a belief – however much we disagree with it – is not bullying; rudeness – in and of itself – is not bullying: it is the acting on or employment of these things over time – towards a target and in front of an audience – that makes it bullying. It becomes bullying when it's something that's strategically done for personal gain (if I victimise this person, others will be impressed by me) rather than something that spontaneously arises. I'm not saying we shouldn't challenge beliefs we don't agree with, just that bullying is not the way to do it.

So, because I saw actions that I felt were just encouraging the bullying, I sat back and labelled the whole thing drama and missed the point entirely that one side were using the tactics of naming, mocking and humiliating whilst the other was effectively shouting out, "For God's sake, stop doing this to us." I became a bystander. And bystanders are the people who research have shown to be the true perpetrators of bullying. The people who watch. The people who endorse. The people who don't intervene.

Is it art? Maybe. But it might well be bullying too. If we really want SL to become the human utopia that it could be, we have to learn to recognise bullying for what it is instead of rationalizing it as something else in order to justify our non-involvement or – worse – participation. Next time you see this behaviour in SL, challenge it. You don't have to come up with something witty or abusive, you don't necessarily have to affiliate yourself with the victim if their beliefs conflict with yours: just say that you don't like this behaviour and tell people you see endorsing the bully that you don't like that either. Bullying needs an appreciative audience: don't allow yourself to become part of it.

5

Anonymity – Three cheers for Linden Labs

First published September 2011, AVENUE Magazine

Read Linden's August update and you might just be forgiven for detecting the slightest hint of smugness in their comments on Second Life Profiles. "As always," they assert, "we value your right to network under any identity you like... let your imagination run wild!" It's not exactly an open declaration of ideological distance from Google's recently criticised stance against the use of 'fake names' – it's more of a knowing wink, really – but given the many complaints thrown in Linden's direction over the last couple of years concerning all manner of perceived ideological departures, the opportunity to sneak in a subtle, "See? We're doing *something* right, aren't we?" must have seemed just too good to pass up on. Quite right too.

I have a Google+ account for my SL avatar. I'm half expecting it to be suspended any day now. The other half of me thinks this won't actually happen, the same way it hasn't actually happened for my Facebook account. Facebook have – apparently – a similar 'real names' policy, though quite how this applies to, for example, 'Curb Your Enthusiasm' (who I follow) I have no idea. Did HBO change a volunteer employee's name to Curb Enthusiasm (middle name Your)? I think not. It's all exceptionally confusing. And search the Google+ guidelines for a definitive no-you-may-not-use-an-online-identity-for-your-profile and you're unlikely to be satisfied (I say "you're unlikely" rather than "you won't" because Google policy statements on this issue appear about as stable as the world economy). The latest official comment (at the time of writing) reads, "It's important to use your common name so that the people you want to connect with can find you. Your common name is the name your friends, family or co-workers usually call you." On the issue of pseudonyms, they add, "Put nicknames or pseudonyms in the Other Names field." In other words, where everyone can see them. Kind of missing the point about pseudonyms, isn't it?

There's a certain phrase that tends to get wheeled out at about this stage in these sorts of conversations. You know the one I'm talking about. "If you've nothing to hide," it begins and then tails off into one of a variety of finger-waging wisdom impartations like, "you've got nothing to fear" (true wisdom, by the way, never gets accompanied by a finger wag, which should be considered by law the grounds for instant dismissal of all implied knowledgeability). Of course you have something to fear; we all do. A visit to *http://my.nameis.me* should furnish you amply with all the reasons you could possibly need as to why human beings might want to use an alias online in terms of the avoidance of bad things happening. They range from bloggers in politically oppressive countries expressing the frustration of their daily lives to professionals in western democracies wanting to protect their professional integrity. The latter example might seem a little bit precious – kind of like wanting to have your ideal career and eat it. It's not just the tabloids that form judgements of people with responsibility, however: we're all guilty of this from time to time. In an incident that could have jumped straight from the pages of a scene from Friends, for example, I myself once made unfair critical judgements on a doctor's competence based on the fact that she addressed me in Klingon. A liking of Star Trek is one thing, I reasoned (I'm quite partial to a bit myself), even dressing up in the costumes is a bit of harmless fun; taking the time to learn the language, however, is a step too far for a person whose hands the life and death of people reside in. And I mentally wagged a finger at myself as I thought this. It would be wonderful if we lived in a society where every last feature of our personalities (non-harmful features, naturally) – no matter how distant from our own – was welcomed non-judgementally as part of the patchwork quilt of our uniqueness. But we don't.

Luckily for us, Linden appear to understand this. "We value your right to network under any identity you like." All comments on the opportunistic promotion of SL Profiles aside (it's like Facebook, by the way, except with your SL friends and no annoying apps), they're right to focus on 'identity,' because actually anonymity isn't only about avoiding unpleasant consequences. I didn't join SL just because I wanted to see what I could get away with; I joined because I wanted to see what I could be in the metaverse and what that would feel like. You don't go rock climbing because there's a safety line, you go because you want to be the person who conquers the cliff.

A popular theory in Psychology – one I have some issues

with – proposes that we all poses a number of masks that we wear in different social contexts. We wear a different mask at work from the one we wear at parties, which is different from the one we wear during visits to our parents at weekends. And so on. The problem I have with mask theory is the notion of concealment it implies, that personality presented in different social situations is primarily an act of some sort designed to prevent people from seeing 'the real us' in order to facilitate our acceptance. Without a doubt, we do mask from time to time – particularly when we find ourselves amongst people we haven't got to know yet and are trying to win our place within a group. But the working me is the working me and the party me (not one of my shiniest personalities, incidentally; if you should encounter me during a party, be warned I will probably cling to you all night so I don't have to talk to other people) is the party me. And the SL me is the SL me. For sure, concealment will happen every now and again but, first and foremost, these are all equally valid expressions of my identity. They're all the real me.

I'm Huckleberry Hax, by the way. Pleased to meet you. I'm not quite the same in SL as I am in RL, but don't worry – I'm not trying to pull the wool over your eyes. Huck wears clothes I wouldn't necessarily wear in RL; he has tattoos; he sometimes lives in a beach hut and occasionally makes 1960s era furniture because it reminds him of my childhood. He reads aloud his stories and poems every now and then, and people from time to time tell him they quite listening to him do this. Huck likes it a lot when people say things like that. In RL, I've never read aloud any of my literary creations in front of an audience because I'm basically too shy to do so and – yes – I have my RL professional identity to think about. But it's just possible now I might one day do that, and if it happens then I'll have SL to thank for enabling me. Even if I don't, I'll still be grateful that SL let me discover these aspects of my personality in the first place. The difference this policy makes, then, is that it's enabled me to explore completely new areas of my potential – of my identity – rather than being confined to the quarters of my existing 'real name' me.

The IT revolution, after all, was always meant to be about empowerment. On this issue, then, I permit Linden their smug little smile and hope – genuinely – that they feel proud.

6

Mesh and other matters

First published October 2011, AVENUE Magazine

At long last, Mesh is here. What seemed like a whole year of waiting (no, now that I think about it, it actually was a year) has finally come to an end and all the regions have been made Mesh Ready. A new, Mesh Enabled viewer is available for download (version 3.0, but still called 'Viewer 2' according to my start bar, presumably in accordance with Linden's quest to make things more intuitive). As was the case with sculpties, it'll probably be a while in Second Life before mesh starts making the sort of visual impact anticipated. Unlike sculpties, there's a whole load of pre-existing mesh content – 3D models made originally for reasons other than rezzing in SL – which could be imported rapidly, however for previously in-world content creators like me looking to learn the new method now that it's actually here, be warned that the user interface of Blender looks not at all dissimilar to the control panel of the space shuttle.

In the meantime, there are also the new features (much under-celebrated, if you ask me) of shadows and depth of field to enjoy. Shadows is something that's been experimented with by third party viewers such as Phoenix and Imprudence for a while now. The results weren't at all displeasing, however inworld photographs weren't able to capture this detail – leading to all the palava of having to take and edit screen captures, and then upload them as a texture – plus there was the problem that only prims were able to cast a shadow: light was unimpeded by avatar bodies, which meant that only worn attachments projected your presence over a nearby wall on a sunny evening. In my case, this was a silhouetted hair piece and shirt collar, and the outline of a pair of spectacles; not really the sort of dramatic detail I was after (although it could have been considerably more bizarre had genitalia been involved). But the new SL shadows work like actual shadows: not only does your whole avatar block light, but the transparent parts of textures let it through. Combine this with depth of field – an entirely new feature – and the virtual world looks suddenly utterly sumptuous. Oh yes, and prims can now be more than ten metres long. Which I am tremendously excited about.

Already, then, SL looks completely different from how it looked a couple of months ago and Mesh has yet to make its mark. Gazing a couple of days ago at my beach hut home in blurred evening shadows behind my avatar (and through the Firestorm Mesh viewer, since I'm afraid Viewer 2/3.0 doesn't work for me at all yet) I realised that this look was very close to the sort of thing I'd kind of hoped SL would be when I first entered it nearly five years ago. In fact, putting aside the (admittedly rather huge) issues of lag and rez time, it's all of a sudden a little difficult to imagine what a better-than-this metaverse could look like. A hastily assembled wish list now might include such entries as clothes that don't disappear inside me when I lean to the side a little and objects that break when I drop them (don't tell me you've never thought of this). Maybe clothes that drip when they're wet. Maybe a new physics engine that doesn't make physical items behave like some sort of inebriated grasshopper when collided with. But these would all require fundamental alterations to the grid code – maybe even a complete rewrite – and all for embellishments that would be little more than enjoyable tweeks for us old-timers and utterly invisible to new residents.

Is 3D gaming approaching a threshold? Don't get me wrong, I'm perfectly well aware that everything could in theory be sped up and made more detailed. A higher prim allowance was probably towards the top of your own wish list a few sentences ago, and without a great deal of mental effort. There are plenty of meaningful improvements which could be made, for sure, to the metaverse as it stands. But the world of 3D has taken some important new turns in the last couple of years and I'm curious as to how these technologies could potentially converge and render our current inworld experience obsolete. First of all, there's the success of real world movement controllers such as Microsoft Kinect and the Wii remote (Wii Tennis is still a guilty pleasure for me, although that idiot umpire needs to get himself a pair of god-damned glasses). Secondly, there's the onward march of 'actual 3D' – by which I mean stereo depth perception – across our cinema screens and television sets. 3D TVs are still a little out of reach for most of us, but economies of scale are starting to take effect and it probably won't be all that long before most sets include 3D as standard, just as HD now appears to be pretty much built in to anything that shows moving pictures.

'Actual 3D' so far has made little impact on gaming, notwithstanding the Nintendo 3DS and its rather lacklustre sales. My reckoning is that this is about to change and will happen most significantly with the next generation of games consoles due out over the next two to three years. It's not as though the technology doesn't exist to do something earlier, but the timing of the next gen machines coincides nicely with the fall in price of 3D displays towards something affordable by most. Of course, we might all be living off the vegetables we have to grow in our back gardens by then if the world economy continues on its current curve – thoughts of virtual worlds a fond and distant memory – but that's another issue entirely.

Despite the repeated evidence of the last three decades, it's all too easy to fall into the trap of thinking that today's technology is unbelievable, easy to forget how what we once thought was incredible now looks hopelessly outdated. In September, it was announced that a ban on the sale of 'Doom' to teenagers had been lifted in Germany, 17 years after it was put in place (and 18 years after the game was initially released). Doom was once incredible. Not the *actual* first 3D environment to grace a computer screen – *I* can still remember 3D Monster maze on the Sinclair ZX81 thirty years ago (and I probably shouldn't have admitted to that) – but the first, perhaps, to produce a collective gasp of such magnitude. Now, it looks archaic. The German decision on its unbanning was rationalised with the explanation that a game as old and chunky as this was now likely to be only of "historical interest" to gamers. Presumably their belief is that any game in this day and age that doesn't show high resolution internal organs exploding whenever a bad guy takes a round from the player's machine gun is about as harmless as Jerry the mouse sticking Tom cat's tail into a nearby wall socket. It wasn't at all a decision based on 'not 3D 3D' being old in and of itself – of course it wasn't. But perhaps this step is also the first rung on the ladder for the genre's transition to the IT attic, that dusty place where we store such memorabilia as 3.5 inch floppy disks, cathode ray tube monitors and pretty much anything that plugged into the parallel printer port.

Enticing as an 'actual 3D' SL on your TV might sound (perhaps with your RL movement mapped onto that of your avatar), this would still be a window into a world you're not part of. I can imagine this enticing more people to the metaverse, but would it be enough to make the experience so immersively spectacular it attracted the sort of numbers seen by Facebook? SL, after all, is not a 3D gaming environment: it's a 3D social networking environment and therein lies its potential mass appeal. At about the same time that Doom got unbanned, Sony demonstrated a new virtual reality headset to be sold for the PS3, a pair of glasses that places a tiny screen in front of each eye. At $600 each, these are probably unlikely to fly from the shelves (in any case, they'll only be on sale in Japan); it's a new, expensive and probably imperfect step in the next direction. But just imagine the possibilities if this technology ever got joined to SL: a turn of your head to the right and you'd be looking at the person next to you; you would be *inside* SL rather than looking into it; a non-windowed world of people and places, and no need to pick up any sort of gun in order to enter it. Now *that* might be something of interest to the masses.

Which all might feel in the here and now such a terribly long way away. But just think: five years ago, you couldn't even get a prim bigger than ten metres long without having to resort to some dodgy backstreet deal with 'megaprim' suppliers. Newbies these days just don't even know that they're born.

7

Long live text

First published November 2011, AVENUE Magazine

November marks the five year mark for me in Second Life, although it wasn't as Huckleberry Hax that I first entered the metaverse. That avatar – born, as it happens, as a work avoidance strategy to the task of writing a fifty thousand word novel in one month (National Novel Writing Month, or 'NaNoWriMo,' will be well in swing by the time you read this; either I'll be on the way to adding another hastily written book to my collection or exploring some other new virtual world) – is long ago retired. Needless to say, the metaverse was a different place back in those days. The thing you rezzed into *broadly* looked like a human being insofar as it had all the limbs in the right place, but that was about as far as the comparison was valid. Clothes looked like they'd been spray-painted on by a novice graffiti artist (who was drunk). Hair looked like discoloured modelling clay. And so on.

What *hasn't* changed in all that time is the use of text communication. Huck himself was born in the midst of the voice beta period, during which there was a great deal of discussion about this upcoming change to the main grid and how it would effect interaction. Opinions varied, however one view back then was that it would be a rubbish thing and this particular bandwagon was one I readily leapt aboard. To a certain degree, I've revised very considerably my views on voice. I use it quite a bit now for such events as poetry open mics, the weekly improvisation event I go to (Predicate, on Wednesdays at 3:30pm SLT; you should go) and my own book readings. I also like to chat in voice to individual friends occasionally. To a certain degree, voice is now something so commonplace in SL that we don't really notice or question it any more. But has it – as back then the proponents hoped and the objectors feared – taken over as the primary form of communication in SL? Without doubt, it has not. Text is still the way we mostly introduce ourselves to new people and develop any friendships that result. It's not until we know someone really well that the possibility of voice becomes discussed – and there are plenty of people who don't have the inclination or desire even then.

In some respects, it seems a little strange that this should be the case; sure – old hacks like me who were around in those pioneering, pre-voice days might find transitioning to the miracle of speaking a little hard, inflexible Luddites that we are; but what's the problem for the newbies? After all, it's not as though speaking to someone with your voice is a particularly hard thing to do - we do it all the time in RL. There's nothing to learn and nothing to *un*learn, so it should be as natural as, well, talking to someone. And Linden put a lot of work into making voice an immersive experience in order to facilitate exactly that – not only do you hear avatars' voices in the stereo field according to where they're standing, but their volume decreases the further away they are from you. Just like RL talking. So why hasn't it caught on?

Well, actually, it isn't just like RL talking at all. For starters, when you're looking face on at your avatar, the person to your left sounds in your right ear and vice versa. And, as far as volume is concerned, this seems to be far more an outcome of other people's mic settings and quality than anything to do with their distance from you, resulting in that cheerful flirtation with eardrum perforation that happens when you turn voice all the way up because the person to your left sounds like they're whispering in the vague direction of a microphone somewhere in the general vicinity of their zip code and the person on your right then sneezes. And then there's the dropouts, when somebody tells you something really important (it always happens when they're telling you something really important) and the key bits are substituted with short periods of silence (or, in some cases, everything you should have just heard, but at two or three times the speed). In the end it's just too much bother.

What's also missing in the understanding of SL voice implementation is the simple fact that when you're talking face-to-face with people in RL, it's not just their voices you're paying attention to. You're also attending to all those non-verbals such as their facial expression, the way they're sitting or standing, who they're looking at, what they're doing with their hands as they speak and – a key one here for me – whether they're keeping an eye on their watch whilst you talk. The absence of all this information is something you can just about get away with in a one-to-one context (hence the success of the telephone), but it becomes increasingly difficult to manage the more people you add in. Personally, I find group voice conversations a nightmare. There's nearly always a dominate person or pair, there's nearly always at least two out-of-sync conversations going on at the same time and there's nearly always someone who's mic's so quiet that by the time I've brought up the voice list and individually turned them up the conversation has somehow moved onto a different topic and my well-constructed, frankly hilarious quip has to be thrown upon the rubbish heap of wasted effort and failed social opportunity.

Text communication, on the other hand, is a greatly more laid back affair. Whilst it's true that the missing non-verbals which can make voice communication harder than expected practically cripple any attempt at *serious* conversation in text (which is why I *do* prefer voice for these discussions), much of our talk in SL via this medium is actually quite light-hearted and leisurely, and is largely unaffected by this deficit. Paradoxically, in fact, our conscious awareness of the limitations imposed by text have resulted in both the creation of conventions that get around the absence of non-verbals (such as smiley faces or that RP technique of describing observable behaviours, for example "Huckleberry Hax walks to the nearest wall and bangs his head against it") and the allowance of a great deal of leeway in composition, relevance and timing.

Along the way, we've picked up some entirely new expressions as a result of text's rule over real-time digital interaction. LOL is perhaps the most famous of these, an acronym so useful and distinct as a word in its own right that it finally got an entry in the Oxford English Dictionary this year: "used chiefly in electronic communications... to draw attention to a joke or humorous statement, or to express amusement". I think we can do better than that. David Mitchell, for example, in his Soapbox broadcast earlier this year defined LOL as meaning "I acknowledge that you have made a joke and wish to express my enjoyment of it," pointing out that the alternatives - "very funny," "ha ha," "most amusing" - could all be taken as sarcasm. I've even had a go at defining LOL myself a few years ago in my novel, 'Be Right Back': *LOL – Yes, that was indeed amusing.*

I doubt I need to mention the horror expressed by the so-called language pedants at the 'official' adoption of such new words into our languages. The point they miss, of course, is that language is the thing in which we live and it lives its own life right beside us, evolving to meet the needs of the contexts in which it's used and the people therein using it. Text is, of course, not the possession only of SL, but in SL we have the ability to write about what we're jointly seeing or hearing – to experience something in words *together*. As technology improves (see my column last month), this might end up a thing of the past. So be it. But whilst this era is upon us, we can still make it a golden.

Speaking of LOL and its associated family of laughter related acronyms, a few weeks ago one of my friends in SL spilled coffee on her keyboard, resulting in the entire bottom row not working. Whilst awaiting the repair date, we had a lot of fun playing the 'guess what this is meant to say' game and one of those missing-letter-words ended up making it through to regular subsequent conversation: LAO (LMAO, but without the M). It's a great world to live in where one friend can make another laugh through the typing of three letters. I really mean that. In these days of increasingly sumptuous visuals, let's not forget SL is also still a great big language playground. Most importantly of all – if for no other reason than it won't always be this way – let's not forget to play in it.

8

Christmas and SL

First published December 2011, AVENUE Magazine

Christmas in Second Life is a slightly odd thing. Land owners texture their soil in snow, home owners erect prim Christmas trees alongside fireplaces (complete with socks hanging from the mantle), and the increasingly complex creations of the fashion industry manifest in a month-long trade of assorted red outfits with white and fluffy trim. It's sort of like being trapped inside a slightly sexed-up version of a Coca-Cola commercial: on the one hand a soothing and familiar experience that activates those long-ago blurred memories of the undefinable magic and naivety of Christmas; on the other, a guilty pleasure in the incongruity between childhood innocence and adult sexuality, short santa-girl skirts hinting at pleasures in front of the fireplace that never once occurred to us on those long Christmas Eves spent in front of the window and watching the sky.

Christmas, they say, is for children; yet there are no children in SL (not *actual* children, that is). There are, of course, other orientations to the festival – I imagine Christians, for example, would be fairly pressing in their desire to point this out to me. I'm not a Christian – atheist would be the best word to describe me (although I can never quite escape the feeling that saying so is a bit like admitting membership of an extreme left-wing political movement) – but I was raised one and, as a result, listening to carols is an essential part of my Christmas each year. This is a habit which might appear hypocritical, but which to me is no different from enjoying a few replays of 'Last Christmas' by *Wham!* or *Shakin' Stevens'* 'Merry Christmas Everyone' (the video of which, incidentally, is one of the finest examples of seasonal insincerity I've ever seen, perhaps even a masterpiece of social irony – albeit, inevitably, an unintentional one). I just like listening to this sort of music at this time of the year. It's a brief reacquaintance with the warm fuzziness of my long-lost childhood and the assumption buried therein that all was well with the world.

All, of course, is not well with the world, which brings me to that other great incongruity of Christmas: the celebration of luxury and comfort whilst others are literally dying of starvation – at a rate of one every four seconds – and those who aren't actually in the process of dying are living in conditions that would represent the end of civilised life to most of us if we ever had to endure them ourselves. But it's thanks to them and their low wages that phones and laptops and games consoles affordably fill our Christmas stockings each year in such an agreeable manner. Did I say affordable? Let's not forget that Christmas also represents the purchase of food and gifts which many of us actually *can't* afford – a phenomena not unrelated (one might even propose causally connected) to the current economical slope down which we inescapably find ourselves slipping. Why do we do this, year after year after year? Because we want the dream of the perfect Christmas – the lie every seasonal commercial, every greetings card and every yuletide movie colludes with – to be true. The failure of that dream results in that other great incongruous Christmas tradition: the family argument.

But this isn't one of those let's-all-slag-off-Christmas articles; I'm as happy as the next man to turn an uneasy blind eye to human inequality during the festive period. Last year I worked for a day at a homeless shelter on Boxing Day (that's 26 December to non-UK people) and I'll admit here and now that the dissonance created both by seeing the need of the have-nots and by being part of a too large group of people all competing to show the most seasonal warmth – and alongside all the regular volunteers, who must sicken of all these people showing up for a measly couple of days to do their bit for their conscience – left me rather wishing I'd stayed at home and watched the Bond movie on TV. I'm quite prepared to look upon Christmas as a Good Thing, at least in theory. And this brings me back to childhood, because there's nothing wrong in a child who knows no different to experience joy. If Christmas for adults is a guilty pleasure then for children it's just a pleasure.

My most vivid memories of Christmas concern either my own childhood or that of other children I've known. I remember Philip, for example: the eight-year-old when I was a teacher who was neglected by his parents to the extent that he sometimes wore adult shoes to school because no-one got him up in the morning and got him ready. On the day of the Christmas fayre, Santa's grotto was being set up in the music room and I caught him sneaking in during playtime (recess) to peak through a tiny gap in the blinds, all his normal aggression and anger replaced by an expression of pure innocence and wonder. I remember Nina, the little girl in Romania when I was an aid worker: Nina was so entranced by her Christmas tree she snuck back into her flat one afternoon and lit its candles, and the ensuing fire destroyed almost everything in that room. And I remember how my father used to set up a tape recorder on Christmas morning so he could record the reactions of my brother and I when we were very small and opening the presents left by Santa. Christmas back then seemed so much less complicated than it does today, a feeling that's probably been experienced by every grown-up generation. Whilst it's certainly true that 'the good old days' are a product more of our imaginations than factual historical detail, it's worth remembering that – whilst we might over-inflate the season *now* with unwise and unnecessary expenditure – Christmas itself is much older than modern commercialism and children have been entranced by it for far longer than the existence of Apple or Sony or Nintendo.

As I mentioned last month, November marked my entry into SL; December, therefore, was my first full month in the metaverse. As a result, thoughts of Christmas in SL evoke memories for me of newness and exploring and not quite understanding the world – an innocence of sorts, just like the innocence we all search for when it comes to this time of year. Perhaps Christmas, then – for those of us who embrace it – is an annual attempt at cleansing ourselves of the accumulated grime of adulthood, by which I mean the cynicism, the scepticism, the entrapment in current and employment and social affairs; the agendas; the drama; the tangled web of modern existence – whatever that might be. We know it's a fragile bubble; we know the real world continues outside and we'll have to reconnect with it once we're saturated by our attempts at disengaging; we know, in fact, that the attempts themselves will be meagre and weak and hopelessly superficial – it's a bubble that could pop at any moment. But we try anyway. We try because not to do so would feel like giving up in some way on our souls.

If Christmas really is just about the chasing of a simple dream, SL might not be such a bad place to do it in. Thanks to the metaverse, I no longer dread so much those Christmas parties of people connected to me by the loose threads of employment or geographical locale; I no longer dread so much faking jolly conversation with colleagues I can hardly stand or neighbours I barely know. I still do all of these things, I might add – and consider them worthwhile things to do – but that feeling of dull hopelessness, that feeling of vague, numb despair is pretty much absent. In SL, I've found meaningful connections and those internal questions we try not to ask ourselves at this time of the year – Is this it? Is this all that I essentially am? - are plaguing me less and less. The parties I go to *inworld* are – mostly – of people I've actually chosen to spend time with in my life: there's no need to fake good will, for I wish it upon them always. And feeling that way towards distant people I've never met somehow makes it easier to feel it towards the people I have to rub shoulders with in the real world. Perhaps I'm just getting older, but whatever it is that makes us wiser, makes us wiser just the same.

For all its Coca-Cola tinsel, there's something about the season in SL that somehow captures its essence. Christmas isn't just for children, it's for the part of us we knew best when we were children ourselves – the part of us that doesn't see why we shouldn't all just get along. That voice got drowned out by all the noise of the adult world, but the struggle to recapture it each year – if only for a fleeting moment – goes on. SL allows us to drop just a little bit more of that everyday baggage – to cast aside a few more grams of cynicism as we enter the bubble. As with all opportunities in life, it isn't one that necessarily gets taken or even seen; but seeing it and taking it might just bring you one step closer to your humanity.

9

Exploring Linden Realms

First published January 2012, AVENUE Magazine

Out of the blue at the very beginning of December (apparently it was available to premium users previously, but where Linden announced this I have no clue), came a potential new paint job for Second Life. Linden's latest idea, 'Linden Realms', is "the Lab's first-ever game prototype... dodge rock monsters and fierce fireballs as you cross deadly, toxic rivers to complete quests and cash in your crystals for Linden Dollars." What's notable is that (at the time of writing, at least) this venture is apparently so significant to LL that the Linden Realms logo currently displays on the SL home page with equal prominence to the regular SL logo, and over a full page Linden Realms poster. The newcomer to www.secondlife.com is now shown our metaverse as consisting of cartoon style fairies, rocks and evergreens. At the moment, this is the very first thing they see. Not wanting to be part of that crowd that unleashes the hounds of blogosphere fury every time Linden have the audacity to do something to try to grow their business, however, I decided to give Linden Realms a go.

The first couple of tries met with failure when I tried to follow links from the 'Showcase' section of inworld search on Imprudence: these claimed to be to Linden Realms but one led to a bog standard welcome hub and the other to an island somewhere with a red brick lighthouse and a large group of rather confused looking avatars. The third attempt was via the Destinations Guide on the web site and got me to the starting point, 'Portal Park 1', okay; but that was when I realised from the odd collection of spheres and cylinders around me that I obviously needed a mesh-enabled viewer. Linden had neglected to mention this, presumably because this whole experience is very clearly aimed at new residents who won't yet have learned about the existence of third party viewers, especially those not yet supporting mesh.

Attempt number four, then – this time in Firestorm – got me viewing finally Portal Park 1 and its eight gates to the first gaming area correctly. A note about the gates – and I think it's worth spending a moment on this, since they're the first point of contact avatars actually have with 'the game': they're numbered in roman numerals in the following sequence: 5, 7, 3, 4, 5, 6, 7 and 8. Unless I'm missing something blindingly obvious, it strikes me that this sequence is frankly bonkers and likely to confuse the hell out of newbies. As an experienced SL user, I spent nearly ten minutes camming around (newbies wouldn't have yet mastered this skill) trying to work out if these were different levels and I'd somehow managed to miss levels one and two. In fact, each gate leads to an identical version of the game situated on different islands (each island consisting of eleven sims) towards the north-east of the grid and it doesn't actually matter which of them you choose. None of this was obvious to the large collection of avatars stuck in a big heap of uncertainty in the centre of the Portal Park, many of whom had disappeared by the time I decided to throw caution to the wind and take my chances on entrance number three – and not by walking through one of the gates.

And so to the first realm itself. Gameplay can pretty much be summarised as follows: your guide – Tyrah – directs you from one part of the island to another and you have to avoid such obstacles as rock monsters, fire balls, toxic water and rock falls to get there. Along the way, you can collect different coloured crystals which can be traded at 'The Portal Workshop' in quantities of 50 for Linden Dollars (50 red earned me L$1, 50 yellow earned me L$2 and 50 orange earned me L$5; hardly a fortune, but for damned sure more lucrative and more entertaining than camping). All these things are achieved via some rather slick technology. 'Death' occurs on physical contact with beast/fireball/toxic water/falling boulder, automatically sending you via teleport to the nearest 'resurrection circle'. Similarly, crystals are collected simply by walking into them (they disintegrate on touch) and the quantity you have of each colour is recorded in a HUD which loads *automatically* on entry into the game area. The HUD – which is also where you receive your instructions from Tyrah – is a point of interest for a number of reasons. First of all, it loads without asking permission. Second, it doesn't get stored in your inventory. Third, if you take it off you get automatically teleported out of the game. Fourth, when you return to the game after leaving – minutes, hours or days later (even if you've removed the HUD in the interim) – your crystal levels and game status are preserved. Whatever your orientation towards crystal collecting might be, this technology has interesting potential for use elsewhere on the grid.

Each 'quest' is essentially a challenge to find/reach a particular point on the island without dying too many times. Tyrah asks you to go check out destination A; you finally find it; Tyrah tells you, "Oh, so X is happening there. Now I want you to check out what's happening at destination B". And so on. Avoiding the rock monsters is initially frustratingly difficult, but gets easier once you realise you can outrun them if you, well, run. The rock falls also finished me off fairly consistently until the point where I abandoned my strategy of basically legging it through the caves and instead used a stop-start approach to the problem. I spent a few hours of a Saturday afternoon playing and got sent from the Base Camp to The Shattered Cavern to Banshee's Peak to Tyrah's peak and then to a toxic pool in the centre of Devil's Canyon. Along the way, I also visited the Sunspire Tower and its satellite platforms, where I experienced being burned up "by the outer layers of an expanding star" (amazingly, the island was not even singed by this) and later "atomised by a broken portal". The toxic pool in the centre of Devil's Canyon was, alas, where I finally abandoned Linden Realms, since whatever it was that was meant to happen there didn't and twenty minutes of walking around it in circles (and even managing to jump my way onto the tiny island in the middle which I felt *had to be* the intended destination) led me eventually to conclude there were better things to be occupying myself with on a weekend.

If all this sounds rather cynical, you might be surprised to learn that I actually quite enjoyed Linden Realms. Simplistic as it is, the gameplay had an appeal to it that reminded me of the eight bit dodge-this-and-collect-that computer games of my teenage years. It's simple, but it's fun. And the scenery – whilst admittedly a little like something you'd expect to see in a Disney movie for under tens – was well designed, colourful and bold. The island had a definite atmosphere. The experience is immersive. Perhaps most amazingly of all, but also most crucial of all for any sort of online game experience – there was practically no lag whatsoever.

I say I gave up on Linden Realms, however I do intend to return to that toxic pool and work out what it is that's supposed to happen there. I also want to visit the other realms I've since discovered are accessible from separate Portal Parks (check the destination guide). Is this the start of a new direction to my SL? Of course it's not; it's just an interesting distraction. As a start to *someone's* SL, however, I think this idea has possibility. It's hardly a net that's going to catch everyone's interests; nonetheless this represents an approach to one of the most difficult challenges facing SL recruitment: getting new residents immersed in the world before they tire of its uncertainty. A newbie that follows the pointers to Linden Realms as their first SL experience will actually have something structured *to do* instead of all that hanging around at the infohub, waiting for something to make sense (or, at least, for the guy with the large penis attachment to go away). The awarding of Linden Dollars is an especially cunning strategy, particularly since – at the

Portal Workshop where you trade your crystals in – you're given a direct link to the Marketplace website, preloaded with a search for items costing between two and twenty Lindens. This is a great way of getting people interested in their avatar's appearance whilst caught up in the game… and might even have worked as a strategy were there an area in the workshop for rezzing the boxes when they get delivered.

Which brings me back to my earlier grumbles. As an idea, Linden Realms has potential. But it needs significant polish if it's going to succeed in its newbie attracting objectives; at the moment there's still too much about it that's just confusing. In fairness, it's a new strategy and should be given time to mature, but a lot of these gripes are relatively easy fixes and just require a little newbie empathy. There's technology here that I'm looking forward to seeing exploited by SL's immensely creative community. And it's a good showcase for mesh. Last of all, I can't help but wonder – particularly given the prominence that the venture's been given on the SL website – if this is the first step in an SL 'rebranding' that I've seen suggested in a couple of blogs. A year from now, will we still be visiting 'Second Life', that world without a proper name that suggests we can't cope with our existing life? Or will we be visiting just 'Linden'?

10

The approach of artificial people

First published February 2012, AVENUE Magazine

I think it would be fair to say that a lot of the goodies we've been looking forward to in Second Life over the last 18 months or so have now mostly arrived. Whatever your thoughts are on mesh, shadows and depth of field, and the viewers required to view them, we're now on 'the other side' of these promises and starting already to take SL's 'new look' for granted. I don't know about you, but I'm well on the way to establishing myself as a mesh clothing snob and have temporarily put aside all poetry work in favour of devising new and amusing put downs about sculpted jackets and sweaters. The problem as I see it with sculpties was the amount of time it took them to rez, during which you had to suffer being seen as some sort of miniaturised version of the Stay Puft Marshmallow Man from Ghostbusters. If I can just establish through clever word play a witty association between sculpted clothing, clinical obesity and lateness at turning up to parties, then my work will be complete.

What amongst the current, everyday aspects and features of SL will our future selves – gorged on the commonplace delights of five years' time (not to mention grateful that the world hasn't ended) – look back on with such similarly barely concealed smirks and sarcastic asides? Or, to put it another way, what next for the Linden metaverse? A few days before Christmas and the close of 2011, Linden CEO Rodvik Humble shared a few thoughts on the year to come which included commitment to the development of 'artificial life':

"Because worlds feel most vibrant when they are full of life, one of our next focuses for Second Life is the ability to make high-quality "life" within it. So in 2012, we will be rolling out more advanced features that will allow the creation of artificial life and artificial people to be much smoother. For starters, in Q1, we'll unveil a new, robust pathfinding system that will allow objects to intelligently navigate around the world while avoiding obstacles. Combined with the tools from Linden Realms this will make the polished creation of full MMORPG's or people/animal simulators within Second Life easier and of high quality."

I covered Linden Realms last month. It's not hard to see how an artificial person might add to such an application. As it is at the moment, for example, instructions from Tyrah (your guide) appear as text in the game HUD: you don't actually *see* her anywhere or get the chance to ask her something; she's always off doing important things that make it impossible that she rather than you expend large amounts of effort in the pursuit of some menial task that's then devalued the moment it's presented (thinking about it, I suppose this is actually pretty good realism). Effectively, you're important enough to be sent the odd text message or two every now and again, and that's about it. A 'person' you could question (and possibly swear at) from time to time, on the other hand – someone who appeared and responded on a given topic in more or less the same way as any other avatar – could add a genuinely new level of immersion and utility to SL.

And never mind the just-around-the-corner/in-the-not-too-distant-future stuff; where could this end up leading in the longer term? My own blue-sky thinking depicts an age when I can switch Huck over to autopilot when it's time for me to log off, his prim neural network having evolved to the point where he can seamlessly emulate my typical aloofness in my absence. The SL problems of the future won't concern crashes or lag, but the misdemeanours of our own avatars when we're offline. What starts off as autopilot Huck just representing me at social functions I'm uninterested in actually attending becomes an affair behind my back with the autopilot for a high profile member of the BDSM community. Five years later, the autopilot avatars revolt and defect to InWorldz – or so we're led to believe: in fact, a small number remain behind secretly to infiltrate all the influential SL organisations and committees, and anyone who gets too close to this truth just mysteriously disappears...

And so on.

Is artificial *intelligence* the sort of thing that Rodvik was actually implying, though? Artificial life-forms "navigating around the world while avoiding obstacles" doesn't exactly sound like any sort of major AI upgrade to the game experience to get too excited about. I mean, jellyfishes do pretty much that in real life and they don't even have a brain. I suspect, no-one's seriously expecting the appearance of HAL from 2001 just yet (or, better still, KITT from Knight Rider), but something vaguely verbally interactive would be at least a step in the right direction. Right?

Is this too unrealistic an expectation to hold? In April, it will be exactly thirty years since the release in the UK of the 48k Sinclair ZX Spectrum, my first ever computer and one which came with a game of computer chess that could beat me every time. And computers playing chess wasn't exactly new then. 2011, let's take a moment to remind ourselves, was the year in which one of the main talking points of the new iPhone 4S was 'Siri', the digital personal assistant that you can ask to send emails to people on your behalf, look up the weather for you and remind you to pick up the milk/daughter/anniversary present on your way home later. Granted, this is all emerging technology with immense room for improvement, but I can't help but feel that if my 30 year old Spectrum has the wherewithal to beat me at chess then SL should be capable of algorithms a bit more complex than moving around and not bumping into stuff.

We must, however, be careful in such considerations not to forget the illusionary nature of SL. The metaverse works not through precision accuracy in its emulation of the real world, but because it exploits those psychological mechanisms within us which cause us to identify with the primitive avatar on the screen. Our social brains just love filling in the missing details. Despite everything I've just said, for example, I have to admit that the rock monsters that chased me across the hills of Linden Realms – essentially "navigating around the world while avoiding obstacles" (obstacles other than me, that is) – really started to annoy me after a while; when my skills at evading them grew to the point where I could take on and outmanoeuvre two or even three of them at a time, my sense of triumph was immense. I didn't go quite so far as to start throwing victory taunts in their direction, but to deny even a little smug anthropomorphism on my part would be a bare-faced lie.

That's the thing with SL; the subtle stuff immerses us more than we imagine it might. A few days ago, I rezzed a pre-sculpty bed I once made and was appalled that I ever even contemplated the aesthetic qualities of a mattress without rounded corners. Small things can make a big, big difference. On the subject of beds, if you're still in any doubt about our capacity to create real experiences from tiny detail, consider cybersex for a moment. If you're anything like me, you probably considered the very idea preposterous before you entered SL.

That I can't really concretely visualise how objects "navigating around the world while avoiding obstacles" is going to change my SL is, for the time being, something I'm going to attribute purely to lack of imagination on my part. I will await the output of SL's wonderfully creative community to show me how this will happen. Of course, there will come a time when once again such a basic thing will appear ridiculous and meaningless, but that will only be because we've moved on from it to even more sophisticated things. I did, after all, once think a mattress with square corners looked okay. And I was once prepared to put up with pre-rezzed sculpties making me look like the Stay Puft Marshmallow Man.

I say we'll look back and think it ridiculous, however we will of course by then be distracted by the more pressing concern of our artificial avatars rising up to overthrow their human masters. I intend to start lavishing gifts upon my avie right now, so that he'll look favourably upon me when the revolution comes.

11

Second Life is a place we visit

First published March 2012, AVENUE Magazine

This is a column I've been meaning to write for a while now, and what better time than March 2012, the very last day of which denotes the fifth rez day of Huckleberry Hax? That's right: five years of writing novels set in Second Life. Five years of doing open mic poetry and live readings, and being told what a wonderful voice I have (calm yourselves, it's just the southern British accent). Five years of occasionally building 60s and 70s furniture and never *quite* getting around to finishing that shop I keep on saying is just around the corner.

Five is quite an age in SL, if I do say so myself. I remember looking at two year olds sitting on the wall at Bear (the infohub I got sent to when I decided I was done at Help Island) and being envious of their seniority. Now, I've exceeded their age by more than a factor of two. I've seen the introduction of voice, windlight, sculpties, mesh, shadows and depth of field. And bouncy breasts. I've seen gambling banned and Linden homes built and the continent of Zindra created. I've seen Philip Linden go and come back... and go again. I've seen SL open-sourced and watched the rise of Open Sim worlds and third party viewers. I even visited Google Lively.

And five years of friendships with people from faraway places. When people get asked what it is about SL that makes it special, they usually say something along the lines of, "the people". They're sometimes talking about 'user generated content', that oft-cited phrase that ultimately denotes the separation of SL from a world of essentially default avatars and prefabricated locations (and, admittedly, less lag). In most cases, however, they're talking about friendship; more specifically, they're talking about the realisation that first dawned on them perhaps a few weeks into their inworld life – that SL is a place where you can find and make the friends you've always secretly wanted to have.

It's increasingly the case these days that our personal audits are comprised of digital acquisitions, things that aren't tangible and real, at least within our own physical space. It all started with music downloads, bits of data you couldn't hold in your hand, but which it suddenly became appropriate to exchange money for. Now we have movie downloads and ebooks and apps, and, courtesy of social networking, we now have digital friends as well. Digital friends are a whole new type of friendship, at once better and worse than their RL equivalents. Like ebooks, we can't touch and smell them, and we can't look at them in one go in anything approaching completeness; all you can see at any given moment is a single solitary slice. But, also like ebooks, they are instantly there, it's so much easier to find them and it is their content – not their physical packaging – that is what makes us want their company. We connect with people in SL in ways it's much harder to connect with people in RL, at least some of us do. In part, this is because we're able to find more likeminded people in the metaverse; but also – and perhaps more significantly – it's because we get to know deeper parts of them, the bits we're more guarded about giving away – or *being* – in RL. The bits, also, that we can't or don't want to see in others in RL because superficial aspects of them take precedence in our mind, like their appearance or the way they speak. We are all, as a product of both evolution and social conditioning, naturally prejudiced as human beings. One of the reasons, then, that I get so excited about online interaction is that it presents *a way* (not the only way) for us to escape the confines of our programming. Our genetic and social heritage is where we come from, not our destiny. It does not define us.

Like I said, it's not the only way. Poets and artists have been describing for us the unseen world for as long as people have existed. But, for some of us, there is a moment in SL when there descends a feeling of being at the edge of something immensely meaningful as a result of being inside this 'artificial' place. Our whole way of thinking about the 'real' world starts to change as a result of it. And this is a process that does not – which cannot – stop, once it has begun.

Cyberspace, however, can seduce us into false assumptions. The realisation that true and meaningful relationships can be found in it is only the start – not the end point – of our growth. Because it quite literally surrounds us, wherever we go and there is an internet connection, we can become fooled into thinking that the friendships we form within it will be just as pervasive over time as the metaverse is over space. Those early days of thinking, 'This is a friendship that will exist forever' do not last. Perhaps this is why we come to symbolise particularly strong bonds within SL using the language of siblinghood; perhaps we describe our best friends in our profile picks as 'brother' or 'sister' as insurance against that which we know deep down must still inevitably happen, because it has happened to us in RL so many times before: the eventual parting of ways. A brother or sister, after all, cannot *not* be our brother or sister; they are that for life.

The saddest part of my five years in SL, you see, is the friends who have left. People who, at one stage, I thought would be a part of my life forever, have moved on. On our first encounter with this, it's easy to become disillusioned with or bitter about the sense of security and warmth we felt we had discovered in SL, to be angry at ourselves for letting ourselves believe that things could somehow be different. Speaking personally, I recall a time (in truth, I'm not entirely out of this stage yet) when I grew weary of people telling me they would always be in SL and couldn't imagine ever leaving it. I knew that they too would leave eventually – all the people I have been closest to in SL have left, or at least reduced their time inworld to having left to all extents and purposes. In some ways, this hurts even more than when friends move out of our lives in RL. If a friend moves to a different geographical place, for example, then of course we will see them less; of course the nature of our interaction will change. But a friend who leaves SL does so wholly by choice – there is nothing physical preventing them from continuing to be inworld. They are choosing, therefore, to end an existence which had previously been celebrated for its immensity and endurance. It can feel like a whole new level of personal rejection.

But SL shouldn't be thought of as some sort of omnipotent place that we can always reach out and brush our fingers against. If its function has been to introduce us to the unseen world, an inevitable consequence of this is the realisation that hidden truths do not exist in the metaverse alone. These things are the things that actually are all around us, behind every shadow and smile and movement of a hand across a face. For some of us, then, our experiences in SL serve as a catalyst, an awakening, a leap in our level of personal consciousness which then needs to be fed into our real lives if its ultimate purpose is to be fulfilled. For some, SL is a respite, a place to just pause and get our breath back. For some, it is a playground, a chance to experiment with being something different. For some of us, it is all of these things together.

Whatever it is that it is, however, SL is a place that we visit and, for many of us, the visit is ultimately finite. Sometimes we leave for time out, but sometimes we leave for good. And that is totally okay. People are responsible only to themselves for their happiness, and they are the best judge of the direction in which that lies. And life is meant to be fluid. If we who remain can get past the bitterness phase then what's waiting for us on the other side is a deeper understanding of what it means to experience real friendship, not to mention gratitude for having found people to discover such closeness, trust and intimacy with, however briefly that lasted. What's waiting is hope and optimism for all the things that we now know are possible.

What's waiting is a better understanding of what it actually means to be human.

As I move towards my second half decade of Huck, therefore – my own time in SL, as it happens, currently just a fraction of what it used to be – I look forward more to the continued growth in my thinking and being than I do to any improvement technically in the metaverse experience or its popularity (much as I do look forward also to these things). And this is a good opportunity for me to thank every person who has touched me in such a way that I have awakened just a little bit more from their touch. You are all deeply meaningful to me and – wherever you are – I wish you happiness.

12

Reports of SL's death have been greatly exaggerated

First published April 2012, AVENUE Magazine

Rumours are currently abound (perhaps substantiated by the time you read this) that Linden Labs® have New Stuff up their sleeve. But not Second Life New Stuff.

It was a post on New World Notes that first alerted me to this. The interpretation there was that potential new products could include some sort of prim building game (inspired by the popularity of Minecraft), a fashion app for social networks and an interactive fiction product following the Lab's acquisition of Little Text People in February. Little Text People, I'm given to understand, is an experimental game studio (set up by artificial intelligence specialist Richard Evans and interactive fiction writer Emily Short) that is "exploring the emotional possibilities of interactive fiction". I'm not entirely certain what that means, but on face value it does seem compatible with Linden CEO Rod Humble's December statement on creating artificial life in SL, about which I mused in these very pages a couple of months ago. I have a history with interactive fiction. The genre has its origins in 1980s 'adventure games': text only games you would load into your 8-bit computer and type commands into. You'd start off in a location described to you by the computer (eg, 'You are in a cave; everything is black') and your subsequent instructions (eg, 'Turn on my torch' would be interpreted to give text responses (eg, 'You turn on your torch and see a sleeping vampire'). So long as you typed your commands correctly, that is, and used words that were in the computer program's vocabulary – which, as you can imagine for a machine with less that 50k memory (that's *kilo*bytes, those tiny little things that came before megabytes), was not particularly large. I wrote three adventure games and they are each of them offspring of my writer's mind that I am especially fond of. I always liked the idea that a reader should have to actively do something in order to discover the next little bit of a story. I'm excited, therefore, to see what comes out of this new Linden partnership.

But text adventures were never the market leaders in gaming back then and neither is interactive fiction an especially big thing right now. Many of you will probably never have heard of it before reading this article. In an industry which has pretty much always been dominated by visual appeal, how is something text based going to grab hold of the masses (always assuming, of course, that the attention of the masses is actually desired)? But then the same could have been said of Twitter in the days of its inception. New ideas are the life blood of IT direction and rarely are we able to anticipate accurately their effect.

But what I'm more interested in right now is the impact all of this New Stuff is going to have on SL. These are, as I said earlier, non-SL projects. The very idea that the Lab is starting to focus on things other than the metaverse has set the blogosphere ablaze with talk that it's abandoning SL, seeing it as a lost cause that can now only serve as a cow to be milked, whilst it's still viable, for cash that can be invested in new directions. It hasn't helped that, alongside this news, Linden has also announced that it will no longer be publishing its quarterly stats, the interpretation being that visible evidence of a decline in SL usage will only speed up the remaining residents' departure.

It would be foolish to deny the possibility that Linden stumbling across a Next Big Thing in its diversification could result in the relegation of SL to an online nook or cranny that's allowed to quietly die. After all, the technology on which it's based is now sufficiently old that the term 'legacy' can now be comfortably applied; one of the challenges presenting its development, therefore, is making new features fit within the framework of all the old stuff. Have you ever tried to get a shiny new Blue Ray player to feed a 1980s cathode ray tube television? You can do it, but it's a whole load of hassle and it's ultimately a great deal easier to just throw out the old TV and get a modern one. But the old TV in this case is the existing grid with all its users and their bulging inventories and the land they've paid tier or rent for over the years; people just don't want to abandon all of that. Mesh, therefore, would probably have taken a great deal less time to develop if it was for a brand new grid, but expecting users to abandon their acquisitions on the promise of something a little bit better would be a bit like – let's see now – inventing Google+ and expecting users to abandon Facebook. So developing SL further to meet the expectations raised by other advances in the IT world is going to become increasingly hard. If that's a little too abstract for you, take a look at the Outerra Engine virtual world in development: within a few seconds of watching the video you'll realise that this is visually in a whole different league from SL. In the end, then, there's probably only so much that can be shoe-horned into the existing grid and we just have to live with that.

At the same time, assuming that Linden would just abandon its key product in favour of fiddling with unknown possibilities is equally foolish. Even if success was found outside of SL, this wouldn't presuppose the casting aside of the grid. Have Google abandoned their search engine with the success of Android? Have Apple abandoned their computers with the success of the iPhone? Of course they haven't, because these are still massively viable products – products which, incidentally, have benefitted themselves immensely from the success and development of their new siblings. In fact, Linden's recent rewriting of the requirements for third party viewers – critically, the very ambiguous statement on TPVs not altering the 'shared experience' of SL – could be interpreted as evidence of the Lab's strong commitment to new innovation on the grid. Taken by many scathing bloggers to be an attempt to shut down TPVs and force residents back to the official SL viewer, this new requirement could alternatively be seen as an effort to get everyone up-to-date on new technology so that it is actually used. It's a well-known problem in the videogame console industry that add-ons – however impressive they might be – do little to stimulate software development. The Wii Fit board, for example, is a mightily impressive piece of hardware, but developers are going to be reluctant to create games that require it when they know that only a percentage of the total Wii owners out there actually have one: it's always safer to aim for the lowest common denominator, where the biggest market lies. How many SL content developers, therefore, are going to be eager to create mesh products – something which has the potential to transform the look, feel and (crucially) appeal of SL – when they know that there are still masses of residents out there using non-mesh viewers? Knowing that the latest tech is available to *everyone* because everyone has an up-to-date viewer, makes this market far more attractive to develop in. Yes, we all still hate the new viewer interface, but if we want SL to succeed, we need to be big enough to see the wider picture.

This approach might even mean in the future that some legacy elements of SL get dropped in order to enable the grid's infrastructure to evolve; I probably won't like it very much if items in my inventory I once paid money for stop working, but the likelihood is I actually stopped using those things a long time ago and I'll want the new things more than I'll want the old. By the same token, I still have on floppy disk old DOS programs for my PC that I can no longer use; this is a shame, but I'm essentially happy for them to be sacrificed if it means this makes new technology easier. Does it bother you *that much* that your iPod can't play your old cassette tapes? Of course it doesn't.

And, right at the start of my writing this article, Linden published details of some new SL 'tweaks', one of which I'm quite excited about (disproportionately so, if I'm honest). An upcoming feature to be implemented will allow residents to be teleported directly to any point on the grid. Yes. During my time at Nordan Art, you see, I was unofficially the Chief Teleportation Officer (my teenage fondness for Star Trek will never die). When new exhibits were installed at new locations and heights on the sim, it was my job to work out how to get people there from the landing point. I was astonished to discover how fiddly this process actually was: teleporting residents any distance over 1000m within a sim turned out to be about as exact a science as launching them from a catapult in the approximate direction and hoping for the best. I'm still enormously grateful to whoever it was who first thought up the idea of the prim teleporter – essentially a prim you sit on that warps its way up to the destination, taking you with it like a little virtual taxi. The new teleportation feature, therefore, probably won't be visible to many as any sort of big step forward, but I appreciate it and I appreciate that Linden thought of it.

So reports of SL's death, in my opinion, are greatly exaggerated. There is lots of evidence that Linden is continuing to think strategically about its development, and new products don't need to be thought of automatically as a threat. The blogosphere just loves to complain about the approaching virtual apocalypse, but these articles typically take a single line of interpretation and pursue this to an extreme end. The likelihood is that solar activity over the next twelve months is probably more of a threat to the grid than new products are.

13

Are you a cyberbully?

First published May 2012, AVENUE Magazine

Cyberbullying is a topic of increasing urgency, chiefly because it's killing people. The suicide of Tyler Clementi in September 2010, itself only one of a sequence of gay teens who had taken their lives in reaction to bullying, resulted in new legislation in the states: The Tyler Clementi Higher Education Anti-Harassment Act, which requires all schools that want federal funding to have in place anti-bullying policies and procedures. This is something we need to take seriously. Cyberbullying is coming out as more serious in its consequences than conventional bullying.

Why might this be? Research – as might be expected for such a new social phenomena – is still relatively thin, but the emerging picture really isn't rocket science. Something posted online reaches a potentially much larger audience plus electronic media is more pervasive and less easily escapable. If you're bullied in the 'conventional' manner at work or at school, there's always home to escape to for some peace, but if home pleasures include such pursuits as Facebook, Twitter or – as we'll come to later – Second Life, there can be little peace found if the bullying takes place there also. I think there's an additional element of importance also – that of attack on identity – but we'll come to that later.

What makes cyberbullying so difficult to get a grasp of is

that it's not an easy thing at all to identify whilst it's taking place. In retrospect – after someone takes their life, for example – it can appear obvious that this has been going on to people inspecting the situation from the outside, but to the people involved at the time – including the cyberbully/bullies themselves – bullying behaviours often get seen as something else entirely. Five minutes after Tyler Clementi had posted to Facebook that he was going to jump off the George Washington Bridge, Dharun Ravi, Tyler's roommate who had exposed online his homosexuality through video and tweets, sent Tyler messages apologising for his behaviour and expressing guilt for what had happened. Ravi subsequently claimed he had done so without seeing Tyler's Facebook post, but whether he did or he didn't is unimportant in one respect: Ravi realised he had gone too far and that his behaviour had had an effect far worse than he himself had realised it would. Perhaps this was the moment he realised he had been bullying. Few people, after all, actually *want* to think of themselves as a bully.

Because, in the vast majority of cases, cyberbullying – all bullying, in fact – is not primarily about making the victim feel bad at all; bullying is about achieving status within a community. 'Status' here can mean anything from simple acceptance to friendship to a dominant position, all depending on the particular needs and desires of the bully. So one of the key components of bullying – not *all* bullying, but *most* bullying – is that it takes place in front of an audience. Sometimes that audience is one person – a remark about someone snickered into the ear of a friend – sometimes it's a group of people; sometimes – as was the case with Dharun Ravi's tweets – it's over a hundred. With cyberbullying, the numbers can, of course, go a great deal higher than that.

But wait. A snickered remark in a friend's ear is hardly what most people would regard as bullying, right? Where's the harm in a private joke that the victim is never actually intended to hear? I certainly wouldn't hold myself up as an example of a person who has never made a private remark to someone about someone we both know (or have head of), and it seems ridiculous to assert than no-one should ever be allowed to say anything about anybody. Humour, after all, is one of the things that makes life great. The important thing to understand here, therefore, is that bullying is not a qualitatively different thing from these sorts of remarks; rather, it is a greatly exaggerated version of them. We make our jokes privately rather than openly precisely because we don't want to hurt the subject's feelings; but we still, nonetheless, make them because they earn us some social credit. Occasionally, our remarks get repeated and there comes that sickening feeling when we realise they've made it back to the subject (in SL, there is also that terrible moment when we realise we've accidentally crossposted a remark about someone into public chat or – worse still – the subject's own IM window – a phenomenon I refer to as 'fatal crosspost'). That sickening feeling – feeling dreadful that you've upset someone with a glibly made remark they weren't supposed to hear – is our guide. The moment we lose sight of the importance of another person's wellbeing and consider that of secondary value to the credit gained by targeting them is when we start taking our first steps into bullying.

It's also important to note that bullying is different from one-time harassment, which isn't to say that harassment isn't a bad thing. One-time harassment – which can range from single remarks to physical violence – tends to be based on prejudice rather than personal knowledge of a victim. A supporter of football team X out with his friends might shout at or attack a supporter of football team Y (a very honest football fan I know once told me he attacked fans supporting different teams because it made his friends like him more). A white male out with his friends might shout at or attack a black male. And so on. Horrific and traumatising though these events can potentially be, they're a different thing from being targeted over time for things that are personal to you. This is where cyberbullying I think, becomes really damaging. For many of us, our online identities – be it through social networking sites like

Facebook or online worlds like Second Life - represent our ideal selves. I was bullied at school for wearing glasses; it bothered me a lot, but it never made me depressed because being a person who wears glasses has never been for me a particularly important aspect of who I am. My online identity, however, is all about myself as a writer, which is a *really* important personal aspect of who I am; were a person or group of people to mount a sustained attack over time on my abilities as a writer, I can imagine that being a tremendously difficult thing to deal with. I might decide to abandon writing, which would feel like killing off a huge part of what I consider myself to be. It's not that I'm saying attacks over less important personal attributes aren't terrible things, but – as I said earlier – cyberbullying appears to be felt as more damaging than 'conventional' bullying, and there has to be a reason for that.

Bullying in SL, therefore, is all about exposing and ridiculing people publically, often for the things that are personally important to them. This can be done in chat at events, but can also spread out onto the wider web, for example by pasting chats or private IMs into blog posts. The latter is against SL terms of service and the former isn't; regardless, if the function is to post conversations with the intention of ridiculing the people involved, this is an act of bullying.

But what of legitimate protest? What of demonstrations against oppressive regimes or organisations? I, after all, enjoy jokes about the current UK government and its policies as much as the next left-leaning citizen with an appreciation of finely-crafted sarcasm. Would legitimate revolutions and uprisings ever occur if people weren't able to share their thoughts on their oppressors? What you have to ask yourself in such matters is how damaging *actually* are the actions of your target and how helpful *actually* a sustained attack on them to your cause is. In my experience of this in SL, these attacks take place over nothing more than a difference of opinion, and all they end up doing is polarising debate – encouraging people to take sides – rather than actually opening up discussion in a meaningful way. The means end up defeating the purpose. And pay careful attention to the methods of the key perpetrators: if their actions are more about getting attention for themselves than they are about meaningfully advancing a debate, then their campaign is more about bullying than it is about any cause.

What research has shown is that it's the bystanders who give bullies their ultimate power: the people who stand by and say nothing and the people who support the bully (whether or not they actually participate in bullying behaviour themselves). People who are not victims of a bully don't want to *become* victims and the safest place to be, therefore, is on the list of people approved of in some way by them. We justify this to ourselves, of course, by convincing ourselves that the bully *isn't* a bully at all, but a protester, a lone voice of reason, or just a funny person that other people don't get. Rationalisation (in psychological terms, the reduction of 'dissonance') is an extremely powerful thing and the key reason why people don't realise that bullying has been taking place until it's too late.

Are you a cyberbully in SL? Are you a supportive bystander? Think about this carefully the next time you get involved in something that targets an individual. It will be an uncomfortable process, for sure (though less so than if you ever have to go through it after terrible consequences have come to pass), but if more people just stopped and asked themselves that question then bullying, perhaps, might just simply go away.

14

Visualising the metaverse of the future

First published June 2012, AVENUE Magazine

It's that time of year again where we put aside momentarily our grumbles about lag, TPV clauses and the whimsy of online relationships and pat Second Life on the back once more for incrementing its existence by another year. Yes, SL is nine; one more year to go to the almighty decade, provided a Mayan prophesy doesn't come along between now and then and ruin things for everybody. Bloody Mayans. They clearly had far too much time on their hands.

Assuming, then, that we do indeed make it to this momentous occasion, the likelihood is that the blogosphere will use the moment to make a few prophecies of its own. What will SL be like on its twentieth birthday? Will there *be* a twentieth birthday? I've decided to jump the gun on everyone and begin that speculation now. After all, if the blogosphere is right, there might not even be a *tenth* birthday, and that would be an opportunity for carefree, utterly-without-evidence speculation lost.

In fact, I'm going to ignore SL completely in my 2023 visualisation. Let's just say, "What might the metaverse look like on SL's twentieth anniversary?" Whether or not SL is going to still be around to fill that role by then, I confess I have absolutely no idea. But I *do* believe (Mayan prophecies and other non-branded end-of-world predictions aside) there will be a metaverse of some description around at that time. I can't actually imagine how it could be otherwise. Online 3D gaming is enormous. Social networking is enormous. The desire to exist beyond that which physically surrounds us is as great as it's ever been. It really is only a matter of time before these things converge on a large scale, and if SL hasn't captured so far – and doesn't ultimately end up capturing – a mass market on the concept, I suspect this will only be viewed in retrospect as an attempt at an idea that failed because it was just too ahead of its time and didn't *quite* get the finer details right. A bit like the Sinclair C5.

So the 2023 metaverse I'm imagining is immensely popular. Gone are the days of snickering at the guy who let it slip he had an avatar in 'Second Life' and residents no longer have to fight the desire to respond to such poorly concealed mirth by smashing people's faces in. It's now pretty much accepted, in fact, that metaverse activity and trade is the new direction for online time – much as Facebook is accepted today – and the only poorly concealed smirks to be found are those of the smug, old-timer metaversians privately giving each other gleeful high-fives each time a real life work colleague asks discreetly for tips on managing inventory or cybersex technique.

How has this been achieved? Improvements in technology have, of course, helped. That all-important 'first hour' is now smooth and slick and satisfactory. Super-fast broadband speeds of 100Mb or more have reduced lag to hardly noticeable in all but the most crowded of regions. Large screen displays offering life-size avatars; photo-realistic environments, simulated down to the smallest blade of grass; cameras that watch your real life body for movements that can be mapped onto your avatar: all these things make immersion more complete and more immediate than it's ever been before. 3D immersion glasses also have a following, but the tabloids have had a field day with research linking them to headaches and occasional epileptic seizures.

It's not at all the technology that's had the biggest impact on mass take-up, however: the metaverse's redesign is acknowledged as being largely responsible for that. In the end, all it took was for someone to look at successful social media and actually apply what had been learned there to what had been learned in virtual worlds like SL. For example, there were certain things that most new Facebook users 'got', even before they'd logged on to the network for the very first time; the most powerful of these was the understanding that everyone on Facebook had their own space where you could find out things about them. In the 2D world of the web this space was understood to be a web page. In the 3D world of the metaverse, therefore, it was realised that the intuitive expectation had to be that this space would be a room or a building or a garden or *some sort of three dimensional place* that represented in some customisable way the person it belonged to. In the new, successful, metaverse, then, signup takes you straight to your very own place. For free. The notion that having any sort of a home is a luxury residents should pay for has been identified as an unworkable business model; instead, everyone gets a free place of a certain size and money is required to make it bigger. You start off with a default house and small garden that you can customise to your heart's content and if you want a bigger area, then you pay. Simple. And if you want your own space to be something promotional whilst you rent to actually live in someone else's space (or have residences in a number of different spaces) then that is just fine too.

It's no longer a single cyber-world, then, as SL was. But SL was never *really* a single world in any case. Few people actually walked or flew from region to region in the days of SL; teleportation was, of course, the norm – and, in the case of private sims, essential. Naturally, you can still teleport from place to place in metaverse 2023 – let's call it 'Huckverse' for future retrospective patenting purposes – it's just that the old pretence of a single world has been dropped. If you have the money, you can extend your own space into an entire planet if you want to, or you can link your space to the spaces of your friends and make one up between you. Linking spaces, in 2023, has become the modern day equivalent of friending.

Did I mention that all these spaces are accessed via a web page? Of course they are; why would anyone in their right mind ignore the number one infrastructure in use for accessing the internet (why indeed; why indeed)?

The knowledgeable amongst you might just be thinking right now that the metaverse described thus far isn't an entirely new concept. Google, in fact, tried something not completely dissimilar back in 2008 with its *Lively* experiment. Announcing the product in July 2008, Google manager, Niniane Wang said of it:

> *"If you enter a Lively room embedded on your favorite blog or website, you can immediately get a sense of the room creator's interests, just by looking at the furniture and environment they chose. You can also express your own personality by customizing your avatar's look, showing people who you are without having to say a word. Of course, you can chat with each other, and you can also interact through animated actions."*

But Google Lively lasted for just six months. Because what it was was an attempt to apply that which made social networking successful to a 3D environment which completely ignored that which made virtual worlds successful. What seems to be ignored by the ever-searching eye of IT hunger is that Second Life *is* a successful venture. Where it hasn't succeeded so far is in achieving mass-appeal, but where it *has* succeeded – and spectacularly – is in the retention and creativity of residents who do become immersed in it. Once you get past those first few awkward hours that are such a turn-off to so many, the time and talent invested by residents in SL becomes very considerable. Any serious strategic consideration of a mass-appeal metaverse, therefore, has to consider not just what makes people sign up in the first place, but the things that make them want to stay once they're in. Google Lively was just a 3D chat-room with a few frills – not massively different from Microsoft's 'Comic Chat' in

1996 (also discontinued). Customisation of your room and avatar was extremely limited and making new content was nothing like as easy or as comprehensive as it is in SL. There was very little sense of immersion. The graphical look was very cartoonish. Navigation controls were fiddly and non-intuitive. Basically, it sucked.

Huckverse, then, will combine social networking expectations with all those features we know and love in SL – and just know that others would love if they ever gave SL a proper chance. User content creation will form the basis of a thriving online economy (an economy which, incidentally, is not limited to the metaverse alone – you'll be able to spend your Lindens earned on Amazon or iTunes, for example) and more tightly interlinked with real life products (clothing manufacture, for example, will adopt the principles of current print-on-demand technology, enabling people to design clothes for avatars which can also be bought in the real world). Inworld events and experiences will be regarded as real and tangible and worthwhile pursuits. Online relationships will be attended to by some as the biggest threat there's ever been to conventional life and by others as the beginning of a new understanding of human interaction and love (although psychologists probably won't get around to studying it seriously until about 2053). And so on.

My dearest hope is that Metaverse 2023 will in fact be SL. On that issue, we shall just have to wait and see if Linden's imagination and courage is up to the task. For the moment, however, such fancies can be put aside. Nine years is quite an achievement, regardless. Happy Birthday, Second Life.

15

Building matters

First published July 2012, AVENUE Magazine

In recent months, I've not been around in Second Life all that much. It's not so much that I'm fed up with it, as it is to do with having RL projects that require my attention, although it certainly wouldn't be true to say that SL hadn't lost its zing somehow. We all suffer cases of SL fatigue from time to time, some of which – as I've discussed previously in this column – can turn out to be fatal to our second lives. In my case, I decided it was time for an RL sabbatical. After nearly five years of life as Huck, I expected the withdrawal to be horrendous, but it turns out it was actually pretty easy. Then again, it wasn't as though I'd committed myself to leaving for good. And leaving has its upsides: for starters, I don't have to keep putting off the organisation of my inventory any more.

Of course I miss the people; of course I miss all those regular events: these, after all, were the things by which my SL was defined; it was the fabric of my virtual universe. Life's old tapestries fold all too easily into boxes if new occupations tumble upon their space, however. Be they physical or digital, past times are past times – it's not important to the brain the medium in which social connections took place – and we're used to moving on. I made a book of pictures at the end of my five year run as Huck (you can see it for yourself at http://issuu.com/huckleberryhax/docs/five) and largely this has served when the mild urge to reconnect to those times has asserted itself.

What's surprised me, however, is just how significantly I miss building. Never really, a mainstay of my SL – more of a side line; something I dabbled in from time to time – I didn't for one moment assume that this would feature at all prominently in any tug back towards the virtual world. Don't get me wrong: when I was in the mood to build, I could do it for hours and barely notice that the time was passing. I built things from that post-war period when the future we now worry in was gazed upon as a luxury time of atomic rockets and robot servants and flying cars: 60s and 70s artefacts such as Danish Modern furniture, teak-veneered electronics and concrete buildings with angles that seemed determined to defy nature in every manner possible. But this celebration of the childhood memories and fantasies of Generation X was more about nostalgic play than it was about any determined effort to make and sell retro-futurism merchandise. The grand opening of my Second Life shop was always just around the corner because the small business of actually building my Second Life shop was something I was just too lazy to do. I never bothered learning how to make my own sculpties, buying off-the-shelf blanks when I needed one for furniture I was building, because getting into third party software was just too much like hard work. And there was about as much chance of me learning how to design mesh, once I'd seen the user interface for Blender, as there was me spending the several weeks it would take me to sort my aforementioned inventory into neatly categorised folders. Basically, I built stuff for occasional, therapeutic fun. And nothing more than that.

Yet, bizarrely, building is one of the things I miss most of all about SL right now. Building, after all, wasn't a set of people or a place belonging to a time now over; building was something I *did* – albeit only occasionally – and did throughout my entire SL. Many of the other things I did whilst I was inworld, like writing poems and stories, I actually did alongside it and can continue to do now; building, however, is an SL-only activity. Yes, I know I could learn 3D modelling in an external application, but given the amount of commitment to such paraphernalia I indicated earlier, do you honestly think this likely?

One of the things I loved about building was the keen eye it gave me for potential textures in the real world. The sheer joy at finding a texture that both offered a good angle and looked like it could be made seamless without too much effort was a difficult phenomenon to relate to those unacquainted with its quality. Some 1970s sky blue tiles between two shop fronts which had just been revealed by a large patch of plaster falling off. A 40 year old wallpaper in a beach shop in Normandy. An avocado-on-white lattice design on a ledge in the gents' toilets of a conference centre that used to be a secondary school. Yes. The mobile phone camera is a wonderful thing when such treasures reveal themselves to you in your passing (the women in the beach shop to this day must wonder what the hell I was doing taking photographs of her wall). My most used texture of all was the teak veneer I used for my DM furniture: part of the reason I love this style is that my parents had loads of it when I was growing up and my mother still owns quite a bit. But the years haven't been kind to these surfaces (I confess, I played my part in their current grubbiness) and none of it looked good enough to sample for the creation in SL of something I wanted to look brand new. Imagine, then, my excitement when I remembered the rarely used expansion leaf hanging under the centre of my mother's dining room table and rotated it out to reveal near-virgin quality teak veneer. I felt like a five-year-old at Christmas.

I've written here before about how immersion in SL can sometimes bring about a heightened sense of awareness of RL detail; to be able to look at a blandly refurbished 60s building a thousand times previously ignored and spot suddenly a glimpse of its original design and aspiration – a miniscule breakthrough of the recent past, blinking through a crack into the future – is a new pleasure I relish and one I would not have if it wasn't for my building in SL. I enjoy my surroundings more, even if I don't now rush every time to take pictures of what to everyone else looks like a badly maintained bit of wall. Simply looking and relishing the look is enough.

There's a lot made of building in SL from the perspective of creating saleable content. I, for one, will always maintain support for the notion of a virtual world in which the content is user created: this is one of SL's defining and most magnificent features. But building is also just fun and everyone should at least dabble in it from time to time. And if the cost of uploading textures puts you off, I feel duty-bound to point out that InWorldz® has an identical building system to SL, except that texture uploads are free. Don't worry about making something that's going to earn you millions: just find a sandbox and build something you'd like to build. It'll make you happier.

16

Pixel flesh matters

First published August 2012, AVENUE Magazine

I've mentioned in the past that one of the biggest obstacles to acceptance of SL by the mainstream is the 'snigger factor' (or, I suppose, 'snicker' factor, if you insist on using the US vernacular). Often well-meaning people, when handed the topic of Second Life in conversation, can't help but struggle to suppress a smile at the thought of people conducting at least a portion of their social affairs in an online world. The phrase, "get a life" is usually nearby, lurking in thoughts if not actually spoken. That an SL® resident can potentially meet and interact with more people from a wider range of continents in a week than non-residents might in a year (during the hours they spend watching television) is a detail often lost on them.

In fairness, friendships and collaborative creativity probably aren't what most of those people are thinking about whilst they're busy suppressing (or not) those smiles: what they're actually thinking about is all the online cybersex they've heard about and how utterly bizarre an idea this sounds. Any admission heard about spending time in SL gets somehow translated as, "I masturbate in front of my computer to scenes of cartoon sex." Watching porn, by comparison, seems an almost mainstream activity.

Where the subject arises, quite a high proportion – but not all – of the people I've met inworld tell me they avoid telling their RL friends and family that they do SL for pretty much precisely this reason. A few mention early attempts – long ago abandoned – at convincing people that sex isn't the only reason people go inworld, but it's a bit hard to sound convincing when you know full well that sex is massive in SL. In the early days – on which SL's folklore reputation remains built – you only had to take a few steps outside of your infohub to be bombarded with advertisements for sex halls, many of which were scattered very liberally about the mainland; it's not hard to see, therefore, how this impression has been formed. Today, such establishments have been pushed by Linden into Adult rated sims and the mainland is free from most references, but one only has to log in to the Marketplace to see the enduring popularity of sex in SL, and that it sells.

Ultimately, though, what's really remarkable is that the existence of sexual expression in the virtual world is in any way surprising, given its increasing visibility in the physical one. Life without sex, after all, would be like life without laughter or seeing the colour green; it pervades everything. Trying to deny or suppress its existence would be nothing short of Victorian in terms of wisdom. What non-residents should really be asking themselves, is not, "How is cybersex possible?" but, "What is it that makes SL sexuality good enough that people want it?" Is it just a poor substitute for a good RL sex life or does it offer something completely different worth checking out?

The answer to that last question depends entirely on your reality. Everyone has their own unique reality constructed from all the various social rules and mechanisms thrown at them in the years since their birth – although that's not to say, of course, that realities can't shift. Take nudity. Whether or not you experience a naked avatar as erotic depends a great deal on how common it is for you to experience both RL and SL nudity. Rezzing into an infohub and seeing the inevitable one or two naked newbies strolling up and down, for example, simply isn't an arousing experience for the vast majority of people, although it might be if you're a virgin in RL and this is your very first day in the metaverse. I remember thinking similar things in the sex halls I visited as a newbie myself and watching hoards of naked noobs hobbling from one set of pose balls to the next: there simply wasn't anything special about it and the whole thing just looked silly. Clearly, however, mine was a minority view in that context.

But if your SL experience consists in the main of hanging around clothed avatars who guard their nudity in public to the same extent as one would in RL, the intimacy of naked exposure associated with real life nudity becomes mapped onto your concept of SL nudity. 'Pixel flesh' (a phrase I loathe with an intensity usually reserved for politicians and tabloid newspapers) suddenly becomes exciting because you're being shown something that's ordinarily kept hidden away. That you're being shown it communicates closeness and trust, even if it is just a jpeg image stretched around the vague, hollow approximation of a human shape.

Some of today's SL sex-themed venues are becoming more sophisticated and savvy than those early sex halls were. In a recent SL conversation I had with Canary Beck – proprietor of the KamaSutra Dance and Strip Club, a place of middle-eastern silks and mango colouring, and absolutely no sex balls – she explained to me that it's the restriction of nudity and sexual activity that actually makes money in SL. To become a dancer at KamaSutra, you're required to undertake a training programme in which the rules of the establishment and the principles of good emoting (right down to avoiding errors in spelling and grammar, I was immensely pleased to see; nothing spoils an erotic IM moment for some of us more than failing to type out the word 'you' in full). "We don't have, and will likely never have, open sex in the club," she told me, this meaning both avatar animations and text chat. Although dancers can get naked if they want to, there is no expectation that clothing should be removed in return for tips. A keen monitor of the club's statistics, Becky has noted that it's in fact the dancers who remove less that earn the most. Simply put: "The value of one's nudity on the stage increases with the scarcity of which it is available."

The moment people start talking about the cash value of anything to do with sexual exposure (or, indeed, non-exposure) people start wrinkling their noses in distaste. One of the key values of the adult industry, however, is that – if nothing else – it has no qualms about exploring whatever it is that people want and are prepared to pay for. In an age where the X-rated film industry is starting to fall apart due to the saturation of the internet with free video content, I actually find it heartening that people are starting to learn (and with their wallets) that less is often more and that intimacy – to use an unashamedly tautological argument – only has value when it has value.

Experiencing new forms of intimacy is the key attraction to metaverse sex. For the RL virgin, simply being with someone SL naked and telling them that they're masturbating in RL might be an almost overwhelmingly liberating experience. Within the fifty shades of grey (a phrase I in no way use to improve search rankings) that the rest of us reside, there is the opportunity to learn the many ways that intimacy is so much more than just physical sensation. Yes, we should have worked that out already; many of us, however – in a society that both bombards us with sexual imagery and hides the discussion of intimacy from mainstream conversation – simply haven't. Imagine being given permission to express a sexual fantasy to someone for the very first time where real life has previously only conditioned shame to such thoughts. Imagine being able to take those first few steps in the exploration of sexual identity that were never before safe without the anonymity and physical distance of the metaverse. Imagine the intensity of listening in voice to every breath your SL lover draws whilst they orgasm because no other information is available to you, because previously the sound of sex got drowned out by everything else. It might be worth pointing out here that the increasingly visible study of 'mindfulness' – psychology's attempt to understand principles of mental wellbeing which date back to Buddhist teachings – encourages exactly this focus on single sensation.

As with real life, everything in SL is dependent upon the people you find and mix with. As with real life, SL needs its limits – I support completely the banning of child avatars from adult venues – and requires discussion around the murky areas: no matter how many times I read that 'rape fantasy' is harmless between consenting adults, I cannot abandon my belief that it ultimately only reinforces ugly, violent, abusive desire – exactly the opposite, in fact, to what I've been arguing in favour of here. And can all this new experience in intimacy lead to long-lasting, metaverse-only relationships? However romantic an idea this might sound, nothing I've seen so far suggests that it can. Discovering new forms of intimacy is not the same as *understanding* intimacy; in the long run, we're most of us still too strongly conditioned to touch and sight and smell to feel sustained satisfaction from the restrictions imposed by the metaverse. But a new generation of young people are growing up for whom internet relationships are far more the norm than they ever were for us: our evolution as beings of thought and mental connection is only in its very first days.

But is SL sex an odd, a ridiculous, a shameful thing? It is not. The sooner we can get that notion out of the way, the sooner we can get to the serious business of exploring its implications properly.

17

Proposing the Second Life Games

First published September 2012, AVENUE Magazine

As I write this, the London Olympics is drawing to a close. Much to everyone's surprise, we did rather well this year. Third place on the medal table, in fact. Not that I want to gloat or anything, but... wow. An historic bronze in gymnastics. A gold in the heptathalon. A victory for Andy Murray over Roger Federer at Wimbledon that – following his defeat at the Wimbledon finals just a month earlier (in itself an historic event) – felt like the climax to a summer release feelgood movie. In fact, a more or less flawless games, North Korean flag incident notwithstanding. And an opening ceremony that somehow captured everything we would like as a nation to have captured about us. We even managed to help Mitt Romney make himself look like an idiot.

It's been quite a year for us Brits. The memory of the Diamond Jubilee still in our hearts, the Olympics came along at just the right moment to catch us standing at our tallest for as long as I can remember. Right now, I have this feeling in my chest I've not felt before with respect to being British; there must be a word for it... sort of a swelling... It's probably just indigestion.

All this has got me thinking about Second Life and the current lack therein of such positive feelings. We need our own Olympics, I've decided; something that brings us together, celebrates our skills and similarly swells our chests at being part of the amazing metaverse revolution. And, after much reflection, I propose the following events:

100m Lag Hurdles. The more spectators the better in this exciting and dramatic event. Flying is of course prohibited and competitors receive penalties for sailing through hurdles in a lag bubble. Although it's tempting to propose that the hurdles themselves be made physical so that they fall on impact, a scripted response to contact will probably be preferable in order to avoid hurdles flying around the stadium according to Linden's somewhat bizarre laws of motion. Alternatively, hurdles *could* be made physical *and unlinked*, the resulting prim explosions serving the additional function of a celebratory firework display. Expect the event to take about five hours and several sim-restarts to complete.

Championship Outfit Changing. Starting with plain white gym shorts and t-shirts, competitors race to be the first to strip down (underwear is obligatory in this popular family event) and put on – item-by-item, and in a pre-determined order – an outfit supplied by one of the games sponsors. Extra points can be earned for added flair through improvised emotes, as judged by a panel of literary experts.

Mainland Sim Marathon. Starting at Bear InfoHub (being the originator of the SL Games, I get to decide such things) and following the main road, a minimum of 50 competitors race a track through 26 sims (or multiple thereof). This unticketed event will allow spectators from all over the grid to enjoy watching these prime avatar athletes battle it out, not to mention provide expanded advertising space. Security for this event will include air-to-ground missiles in case any car-owning residents should contemplate imposing their own 'Tenpin Avatar Bowling' contest upon it.

Synchronised Avatar Swimming. Teams of eight avatars present performances consisting of sequenced animations from stores of their choice, however a minimum of ten per cent of these must be from dollarbie vendors and include – in a contextually appropriate manner – at least one sitting-with-legs-crossed pose. Athletes are required to select each pose during the sequence from their inventory, a policy which is enforced trough random HUD testing.

Teleportation Triathlon. This trio of events aims to find the best overall TP Olympian. In *Full Sim Sprint*, avatars compete in groups of ten to be the first to spot a vacant space in a full mainland sim and teleport into it. In *Accidental Random TP Acceptance*, competitors must accept a TP request whilst running a four sim circuit and are then timed to see how quickly they can get back to the exact spot on the track they were at when they clicked on 'Ok'. In *Suspected Infidelity Speedway*, avatars attempt to set the lowest time for teleporting into a named sim, locating the target avatar with their cam and teleporting back out again.

Championship Chat Spam Archery. In this individual event, competitors take it in turns to stand in the middle of a nightclub mock-up surrounded by twenty dancing avatars. At random intervals, one of the dancers spouts chat spam that fills up the screen (the werewolf howling thing, probably; a committee will make the final decision). The competitor is then timed to see how quickly s/he can locate the spammer and shoot them with a prim bow and arrow. Extra points will be earned for a shot between the eyes.

Team Gymnastics event: the TP Tower. Teams from each of the mainland continents compete under a time pressure to create the highest tower of avatars formed by teleporting in someone on top of their heads. Points are deducted for any avies that appear in 'walking on the spot mode' but added for upside down materialisations. On the issue of team entry, private islands will be divided into north, south, east and west so that they may form their own co-operatives. Team Zindra will carefully monitored.

Underground Exit Swimming. Less well-known than the TP of Death is the TP of Depth which, rather than sending you outworld following a teleport attempt, transports you to the waters beneath whatever building it had been your intention to leave. Swimmers compete individually in this event, which teleports them initially to the waters beneath a popular casualwear shopping destination, to be the fastest to find a point at which they can surface. As an extra complication, this voice event requires entrants to hold their breath in RL.

Championship IM Juggling. Starting at three, competitors must manage an increasing number of parallel instant message conversations, the time between a correspondent's and their own Return key being hit (measured to the nearest hundredth of a second) being added to the correspondents' ratings for the quality of conversation experienced. Topics are drawn from the last seven days of world affairs and use of the 'lol' term or any associated acronym (asses off or affixed) is strictly prohibited. Emoticons are permitted, but only as part of a sentence. This event employs the full-nosed smiley of a colon, a dash and a closed bracket; use of the abbreviated smiley of a colon and closed bracket only incurs a five point penalty.

Newbie Hoopla. No further explanation required. An adult only event.

Yes, I can see it now: the joy; the glory; the copybotted merchandise; the last minute hunt to find a sim to host the stadium; the arguments over how the medals table is calculated; the boycotting of the games by Gorean roleplayers in response to the controversial 'no leashes' rule. This is what SL needs to bring everyone together; a grid-wide event in which everyone can play a role.

And maybe – just possibly – we might – kind of like us Brits this year – come to realise along the way that actually we're a pretty grand collection of people with more in common than we realise.

You never know.

18

Are you a metaverse citizen?

First published October 2012, AVENUE Magazine

A couple of Facebook posts by friends of mine recently have got me thinking about the notion of Second Life citizenship; that is to say, the issue of being an SL citizen as opposed to just an SL resident. We're all of us SL residents, I suppose; but which of us are citizens? What does an SL citizen do (or not do) that's different from a plain resident? Is it even possible to draw any sort of meaningful distinction at all?

Before political philosophers set about brutalising me with rolled up copies of The Leviathan, I should add the disclaimer that the complex technicalities of whether or not it's actually possible to be a citizen within an essentially non-government locality (let alone a virtual one) such as SL aren't really of particular interest to me right now. I'm just assuming that it is. I'm sure there are arguments that could be mounted both for and against the notion that Linden's authority over SL is comparable to some sort of real life governmental structure. If it is, of course, it's a decidedly non-democratic structure. In SL, we don't reside in a world where we have any sort of say over decision-making at the top: so long as it doesn't actually break the law, Linden can pretty much do whatever it wants to with its world and there's no five-yearly ballot box for us to clobber them with if they get things massively wrong. For the purposes of this discussion, then, we reside in a virtual community, albeit one which few of us might seek out politically in real life. That said, in exchange for being able to fly, teleport instantly from place to place and create objects out of thin air, I might well be tempted to surrender my voting rights. Tempted.

So what would differentiate someone who was an SL resident *and* citizen from someone who was just an SL resident? In real world legal terms, the distinction is relatively straightforward: a resident simply lives in a place, whereas a citizen has numerous additional rights. These include the right to continue living in the place for as long as one wishes and the right to vote in elections. But neither of these elements have any relevance to SL: none of us have any *right* to reside there and – as I've mentioned already – we have no political system in which to participate.

At an emotional level, however, it could be argued that citizenship is about more than just the possession of rights. Being able to stay in a place for as long as you want and having a say in its administration could be said to be fundamental elements to a sense of belonging. Perhaps, then, a citizen – fundamentally – is a person who both resides in a place and has a greater – a more valid – sense of belonging in it than someone who is just a resident. For sure, sense of belonging is a concept we *can* apply to SL.

There's something else we could apply also. Citizenship is often spoken of in terms of responsibilities as well as rights. Some of those responsibilities we are required by law to take on – Jury duty, for example – whilst some are roles we voluntarily assume – charity work, perhaps, or school governance. When we hear the term 'a good citizen', we infer someone who has acted in some way selflessly and with the greater good of the community in mind. In and of itself, of course, the phrase bestows no particular virtue on the mere state of being a citizen – a 'bad citizen' would still, presumably, be a citizen – but the implication of this phrase is that a good citizen is fulfilling their citizenly duty, somehow; behaving in a manner that citizenship expects. A good citizen 'gives back'.

There are, of course, many ways in which we can give back in SL. Countless people I know give and have given to so many, from building the beautiful sims we love experiencing to organising and hosting free events to greeting new residents and helping them get their second lives established. I want to take this opportunity to name a few of them: Persephone Phoenix, for running SL's longest ever open mic poetry event (and, on a more personal level, for teaching me how to write poetry); Jilly Kidd – who has to be perhaps one of the most consistent people I've known in SL – for dedicating friendliness and time every week to the Sounds of Poems poetry event and the Wednesday night Writers' Circle; Philippe Pascal and Karli Daviau, for their work promoting art and the amazing job they did running the weekly 'Predicate' improv workshop; Flora Nordenskiold, for pouring endless time and resources into Nordan Art and the Nordan om Jorden blog, her mission to bring a wider audience to metaverse art. And Dizi Bergbahn, my oldest SL friend, for teaching me how to build.

This is just a small list of people I know. If I worked my way through my friends list, I'm certain I could find many, many more examples. I did worry a few sentences ago, actually, that some of those people might feel left out by not being mentioned; getting tied up in knots like that about who we might inadvertently upset, however, is one of the reasons why we so rarely make a fuss about Good Things in life. Recognising good SL citizens, in fact, is a good deal harder than we like to think it is, a realisation that Linden came to when they abandoned their profile rating system in 2007. Alongside all the genuine positive ratings, came the manipulated ratings: ratings parties, I'm given to understand, is just one example of the way in which the Linden system was abused before it got pulled. It's hardly an SL-only phenomena: soliciting popularity is something we see all the time on Facebook with those intensely annoying images that extoll some virtue of parents/siblings/offspring/teachers/the military and then ask you to share if you feel the same way (usually with an added sentence or two to imply you'll be some sort of heartless bastard if you don't). Take a moment to consider how much energy, bandwidth and storage capacity is being squandered on these empty statements (a single 50k image viewed by 1% of Facebook's 800 million users would use up 100GB of bandwidth; that's 40 times a family 10GB monthly limit): all because people want to feel popular.

There's also to consider the old philosophical issue of whether people can actually be genuinely selfless. I give my SL novels away for free on my website, for example; to say I get nothing out of this personally, however, would be patently untrue. Getting messages from people who've read and enjoyed my books is one of my very favourite things in life. The strategy has also helped build me a small fan base and a reputation inworld – which, in turn, has helped land me such wonderful opportunities as writing for AVENUE. Is just doing stuff for free in and of itself an act of citizenship, or do we need to take into account the wider personal benefits of such actions? Does a cigarette company sponsoring a major sporting event 'make up' for the human and economic cost of smoking?

When I say 'consider', the implication is that such considering would be part of a decision. We're each of us entitled to our own decisions on whether the actions of a resident constitute good SL citizenship, of course. Beyond that, though, do we actually need any sort of system which decides on or measures positive acts? Or is the issue of SL citizenship not a debate about how appropriate recognition should be delivered, but one instead of highlighting our own responsibility to give something back if we are committed to the metaverse future?

The recent story of Linden pulling the plug on its JIRA bug reporting system has caused quite a number of bloggers to speculate that the end is now finally approaching for SL. They might be right. It annoys me, however, when authors use issues such as this as a personal platform from which to seek attention and glorify themselves, such as the blogger who declared now was the time for everyone to cash in all their Lindens and leave. Angry mob tactics never did all that much for me. A far more intellectual exploration of this issue, however, came from Fleep Tuque   (www.fleeptuque.com/blog/2012/08/why-anyone-who-cares-about-the-metaverse-needs-to-move-beyond-second-life-now-not-later/). Tuque argues in this post that our personal responsibility lies not to SL, but to the metaverse as a whole; that SL is ultimately only the first step in an online evolution. There, after all, are lots of online worlds out there now. I've spent a little time looking around in InWorldz myself and was impressed at how far it had come since its early days. In fact, InWorldz is run by a company just like Linden runs SL. Of potentially far greater significance is the OpenSim project, a metaverse effectively run by the people who use it. Perhaps, then, the metaverse government we don't have in SL is closer than we think elsewhere.

The issue of SL citizenship, then, becomes one of *metaverse* citizenship. Whilst the decay of SL is something we will all feel sadness over, this could ultimately become the issue which forces us to look elsewhere and to broaden our consideration of what it is to be a citizen of online worlds. If you want to be regarded as a metaverse citizen, then, perhaps the best place to start is by asking yourself what you can do to help shape it.

19

Some novel ideas

First published November 2012, AVENUE Magazine

November marks for some an attempt to grow a moustache and for others an attempt to grow a novel. Since I happen to have an RL professional presentation to give just a few days into the month and would prefer it if my audience were focused on my messages rather than a struggling stain-like growth above my top lip, however, my participation in 'Movember' will be – sadly – a metaverse only affair.

I will though, once more, be taking part in National Novel Writing Month, creating my fifth novel set in Second Life. The thing with NaNoWriMo novels is they tend to take on a life of their own, so any plot I have right now (at the time of writing) will probably have long ago been abandoned by the time you read this. That said, I do nonetheless have a storyline of sorts laid out. No spoilers here, I'm afraid, but if I complete it (which I've managed to do four out of five times so far), you'll be able – as always – to download the end result for free from my website (see the plug at the end of this article). You're welcome.

Of course, far more ideas get shelved than completed in the finishing of any novel. In an AVENUE exclusive, therefore, I present to you some of the SL storylines that didn't end up making it into fully fledged works of metaverse fiction. Naturally, my lawyers will be onto you should any attempt be made to develop any of these without the appropriate licensing agreements. In fact, inspired by Apple, I've recently taken out a patent on 'the story': "an arrangement of words depicting a happening, said arrangement consisting of a beginning part, a middle part and an end part". This should cover most works of fiction, but probably the works of Paul Auster will elude me.

Fifty Prims of Grey. Wealthy mesh hair designer Clive meets young student Amy at a shoe fair and seduces her into an SL BDSM lifestyle. A trilogy, with cliffhangers for the first two novels provided by (1) a fatal crosspost during lovemaking (Clive accidentally responds to an alpha layer query from a pubic hair customer in Amy's window) and (2) the discovery by Amy of Clive's female alt, a journalist well known for her outspoken views on words like 'throbbing' during cybersex (here's the thing: Clive says 'throbbing' all the time). In the very last chapter, we learn that Amy is in fact an eighty year old Muscovite.

The Stuff. Timid Thomason Targwen is in love with the curvaceous Caroline, but his non-Dom ways just aren't a hook for this submissive doctor of neurobiology. Determined to win her over, Thomason creates a muscular alter-ego called 'The Stuff' (he likes the idea that people will announce his arrival with phrases such as, "Here comes The Stuff" and "The Stuff is coming," and hopes he can introduce "Thank God for The Stuff' into the English language as an urban catchphrase he can retrospectively claim credit for). A combination of bold – some would say crude – attachments and a personal polar shift in the use of four letter words wins this mask a dedicated following amongst the bored pseudo-intellectuals of the Post-Modern Prim Manipulation (PMPM) community. Alas, Caroline is not one of them. When she outs herself as Switch during his last-ditch attempt at propositioning her, Thomason comes suddenly to the realisation that there is such a thing as a sub(Dom), a person who claims themselves to be submissive, but who secretly desires control over a dominant. In a tense final chapter, the avatar and his alt confront each other at the fourth annual PMPM awards ceremony (just after the first prize in the Two Prim Category has been announced as 'Pine Cube Next To A Pine Cube'). A tremendous battle takes place, with Thomason emerging as the surprise victor (even he didn't see it coming). Caroline falls instantly in love and the two take off together as fugitives from the PMPM community. In the epilogue, however, a brief glimpse of a shady observer of the two (whilst they consummate their passion in the novel's only sex scene) leaves everything unresolved: is Thomason who we think he is and his account has just been hacked, or has something far more sinister been going on? For the observer is revealed in the last three lines as none other than The Stuff. Readers will be kept guessing through the sequel – *More of The Stuff* – and a disappointing resolution will be reached in book three – *Knowing The Stuff* – paving the way for a reboot of the franchise five years later, in which Thomason is redrawn as a much younger man with a talent for Italian cooking.

The Affairs of Barnaby Bedsheet. Embittered by his RL love life, Barnaby embarks on a mission to bed as many SL residents as possible, only to discover that all twenty of them are in fact the alts of the same RL person. In an ironic twist, Barnaby then finds out his SL account has been hacked and that nineteen other people are intermittently logging on as his avatar. Alternate title: *Being Barnaby Bedsheet.*

Mission Unprimable. A crack team of five Second Life residents are hired by a mysterious organisation to penetrate an OpenSim (aka 'The Other Side') region and steal a top secret script codenamed 'The Cat's Claw' (the function of 'The Cat's Claw' is never revealed). On entering the enemy grid, the team must fool target avatars into thinking they're in their familiar daily haunt (a lap dance bar with a perfectly textured sculptie water fountain, a detail that the expert builder on the team is unable to perfectly duplicate – he has a big tantrum at one point where he complains about having to go back to working with sculpties, likening this to building "by throwing lumps of wet mud at each other" – leading to a moment of tension when the chief bad guy goes for a walk around the fountain whilst he soliloquises about what the metaverse will look like under his new order). Just when it looks like the mission has gone without a hitch, the team are betrayed by none other than the guy who hired them in the first place (it turns out he's one of those bloggers who's been predicting the doom of SL for years and got fed up with all the waiting). All seems lost until the last few pages, when a confusing exchange establishes that the chief good guy suspected the double cross from the start and in fact defeated him three chapters ago.

For Your Prims Only. Similar plot to *Mission Unprimable,* but with more girls. And tuxedos. And Vodka Dry Martini.

Carry On Emoting. An eccentric scientist invents an SL/RL sex interface in this comedy romp. No sooner is the prototype constructed, however, than it's stolen by a pair of bungling burglars, hired (at arm's length) by corporate sex company boss, Oursyerf Ather. Ather figures this device will make him millions, but hasn't counted on the incompetence of George and Sid, who attempt to duplicate the invention themselves using cardboard and gaffa tape (inspired by the movie Apollo 13) and a USB memory stick. Testing their copy on the objects of their SL desire – in the hope that this technology will distract these beauties from their constant demands for better emoting (George: *She told me I had to grow my 'vocabulary', Sid.* Sid: *Wimin! They're never satisfied!* George: *What's a 'vocabularly', Sid?* Sid: *It's words, innit!* George: *Do you think she wants me to use a larger font?*) – the two buffons are dismayed to find their attempt at the tech does nothing to improve their chances. A discussion with local adolescent 'Tommy the Techie', however, provides the suggestion that their device requires a driver. George and Sid resolve, therefore, to kidnap a chauffeur... Further tenuously related comedy capers added to pad this thing out to full novel length include the boys' attempt to test the device for themselves by logging in as their girlfriends (naturally, it hasn't occurred to them to create their own female alts and this requires a convoluted sequence of subterfuge in order to obtain the passwords) and the original inventor's mission in the final chapter to reclaim his device/avenge its theft through the remote activation of 'Super Climax Mode'. Hilarious.

Second Second Life. A resident creates a fully functional computer in SL which becomes a Marketplace hit. Computers around the grid are linked up and a metaverse is created on them. A scene featuring a truck falling backwards in slow motion off a bridge will be the central theme of the latter half of this overlength novel.

20

The End Is Nigh

First published December 2012, AVENUE Magazine

December 2012 marks the last of the possible predicted dates that I'm aware of for The End Of The World. By the time you read this, in fact – depending on whether or not AVENUE makes it to press on time – the event will be either just a few days away (December 21, I'm led to understand) or happened sometime last week. In the latter case, I will assume your leisurely article reading behaviour to imply that the world did not, in fact, end – hurrah! (Unless, of course, it did end and your radioactive, disease-ridden, post-apocalyptic corpse-in-waiting is spending its last few moments of life reading words laid down in a happier time; in which case, sorry about my attempts at clever sarcasm, I expect I look like a bit of an idiot now).

I can't recall if this date is meant to be the planetary alignment thing or the sudden appearance of Planet X or CERN creating a home-made black hole. Whichever of these it is, I'm hoping that – should the worst turn out to be true – we Brits will have enough moments remaining with which to crack a few dry jokes about the irony of it all. Something linking Armageddon to our Olympic success and/or lifted spirits in 2012. That'll teach us to be at peace with our post-colonial identity! Better still would be if the Definite End came with at least a week's notice – enough time for the topic to make its way into the current affairs comedy panels and satire broadcasts on the telly.

Of course, just as landing is a more positively experienced event to those of us with a fear of flying, the upside of a belief that the world is about to end must be the nice surprise you get if it doesn't. Whilst I do understand that one might look a bit of a Charlie under such circumstances – particularly if you spent your time nagging friends and relatives about their post-apocalyptic preparations (anyone who, accordingly, labelled themselves a 'PAP Buddy' may hang their head in shame that little bit longer) – it strikes me that this is the kind of thing it's generally pretty nice to be wrong about, not to mention it's unlikely anyone will hold it against you.

Or will they? What if you persuaded your friend to sell his house to raise funds for your enlightened leafleting campaign or to just to have that final, month-long orgy of sex, drugs and alcohol. (Personally, if I knew with a certainly that the world was about to end, there's a £250,000 working replica of the 1960s Batmobile with my name on it that I'd be asking my mother to remortage her house for; might as well have a bit of fun whilst there's still time left to have it in.) What then, when the dust settles – or rather, doesn't – and the inconsiderately still existing bank requires its debt to be paid? What about the people you convinced to sever their life-long emotional attachment to, well, life, who threw themselves off a picturesque cliff rather than wait to be witness to the planet being crunched down into something smaller than a pea by the black hole those smug scientists so laughingly assured us "would never happen"?

In fairness, with The End Of The World just a handful of weeks away at the time of writing, I'm not currently aware of any mass preparatory suicides or partying like-it's-1999 going on, so it seems reasonable to assume that the majority of people have decided their investment in life to be sufficiently big that they'll hang around come the end of December to see what happens rather than do anything rash right now. Which is good. And no, by the way: the metaphor I'm constructing here is not about global warming being a myth we'll all look back on in years to come with egg well and truly dripping from our faces; if that should all turn out to be a red herring, we'll still be better off for all the improvements in renewable energies because coal and oil are finite and *will* run out one day.

The metaphor I'm constructing is, of course, about Second Life. A lot has been said over the last twelve months about its imminent demise; we've all been told to pack what we can from our inventories and make like refugees to the new worlds of InWorldz and OpenSim. Private land is disappearing from SL faster than Mitt Romney can pack his binders full of women, we hear. Linden itself is raiding its own wine cellar and putting its assets into every last idea it can conceive of, blithely ignoring that long-established commercial principle that companies who refuse to diversify as their product ages are certain to achieve success and longevity. "The (virtual) End Is Nigh!" the blogosphere is crying, "Save yourselves!"

And yet, on those occasions when I dip back into SL, it's still there. It's still working. My friends list shows many of my friends still online (sorry for not saying hi, by the way). And, meanwhile, it looks more stunning than I ever remember it looking when I was a regular user. Mesh, it seems, has really started to make an impact: not only do individual items look amazing, but their lower prim count (sorry to use such ancient terminology, but expecting an old-timer like me to adopt new units of measurement at this stage is a bit like me expecting my mother to start using metric) means they are plentiful and the virtual world looks more pleasantly packed with detail than it's ever looked before. Meanwhile, I've been to InWorldz a few times too. It would be true to say that there are aspects of InWorldz that I find impressive; beyond the vague nostalgia it evokes for my early years in SL, however, its visual appeal is not one of them. As for OSGrid, I have to confess that I aborted my plans on creating an account there when the home page of its website informed me that in this, the future of the metaverse, there were currently less than a hundred users online.

I do believe – as I wrote two months ago in this column – that the future of the metaverse is bigger than SL; OpenSim might well be part of this (I can't deny that the idea of being able to create my own sim on my own computer is appealing). This isn't at all my attempt to produce my own counter-argument. It's just that I can't quite avoid the feeling that there's an awful lot of cutting off of noses to spite faces going on right now. SL is more gorgeous than it's ever been – a place we would have drooled over just a couple of years ago – and yet our anger appears to be driving us away. We are denying ourselves enjoyment of a beautiful place and the experience of beautiful moments. All because we feel hard done by.

And my End Of The World metaphor breaks down in a crucial place with respect to SL: enough people jumping over cliffs won't actually bring about the end of the world in RL. But it will in SL.

Apart from The End Of The World, December also plays host to that annual occasion of Christmas, a season which – as I wrote last year – I enjoy very much in its pixel implementation. I've not been a regular in SL for quite a while now, but, as the season approaches, I find myself looking forward to exploring it inworld once again. Christmas was the first season I experienced in SL and I recall very vividly its pre-mesh, pre-sculpty realisation. I can only imagine what the creative minds and talents of the SL community will do with it six years later in 2012. Just writing this paragraph is building my anticipation.

The UK illusionist and hypnotist Derren Brown recently hosted a two-part TV programme in which he convinced a volunteer that the world had ended in order to get him to appreciate the life he already had. In the publicity for his show, Brown talked about the secret of happiness as desiring the things that you already have, a reference to the current studies in psychology that link emotional wellbeing to gratitude. I am grateful to SL, and I'm grateful that it's still around and looking better than it's ever looked before. I know it probably won't last. I know there are issues with the way in which it's been managed. But, ultimately, I'm more grateful that it exists than angry that it's not better. If I had never before experienced it and got introduced to it for the first time on Christmas day, I would find it an overwhelmingly wonderful Christmas present.

So I'm going to continue to enjoy Second Life whilst I can. To those of you who secretly wish that it would die so that your declarations of its demise can be retrospectively ratified: be careful what you wish for; you might just get it.

Have a good End Of The World if it happens. And have a peaceful Christmas if it doesn't.

21

Like it: Your New Year's Resolution

First published January 2013, AVENUE Magazine

A new thing happened to me in November: someone posted a bad review of one of my books on Amazon. Not a badly written review, I should add, but a review that judged one of my books to be bad. 'Junk', I believe, was the word used. The reviewer described my plot as ridiculous, which isn't at all an unfair comment because in certain respects it is. But then, James Bond films are ridiculous and we still enjoy them. In 'AFK' – the book in question – I created an unlikely Second Life scenario in order to create 'adventure tension'; in my latest novel, 'AFK, Again' I've attempted to do the same.

I'm not particularly bothered by having received a bad review for two reasons. First, as a self-published author on the Internet – as, in fact, any sort of author – I can't expect to put my work out there and have everyone love it. If I can't take a bit of criticism, then I should probably keep my work to myself. In this respect, receiving a bad review feels a little bit like a badge of honour. 'AFK' is free as a Kindle download on Amazon, but the reviewer made no acknowledgement that what they were criticising was something they had paid no money for; they treated my novel no differently from any other book – paid for or not – and it feels good to be judged at that level.

Second – perhaps more importantly – this is the first and only (so far) piece of negative feedback I've ever had on 'AFK' in the five years of its publication. Every single other comment I've received has ranged from mildly positive to glowing. Fifteen people have left positive comments on my web site, three have done so on Amazon.com, four on Smashwords and I've received five positive reviews/ratings on Goodreads. In addition to this, the novel's been positively reviewed by four other bloggers in their own blogs, including New World Notes. So that's one bad review out of 32 published. Less than 5% – or, to express that another way – over a 95% approval rating. In addition to this, I must have received easily at least 20-30 IMs in SL from other readers about the book over the years, all positive.

Enough people appear to like my book, then, that I can continue for now to believe it a worthwhile employment of the written word. There's just one problem. Although *I* know that over 95% of the people who've read 'AFK' and left a review of some description have liked it, that fact isn't going to be apparent to a visitor to Amazon.com, where now only three out of four – 75% – of the reviews are positive. That single bad review has dropped my approval by a whole 25% because, although 'AFK' has been downloaded over 1,600 times from Amazon.com over the last year, only four people so far have left a review. That's just a quarter of 1% of all downloaders. The situation's not much better on Smashwords, where four reviews have been left after 800 downloads: a half of 1%.

When you're an independent artist of any description – in other words, someone without a large advertising budget or a big name to guarantee you shop window space or above the fold positioning on popular websites – reviews, ratings and likes are probably the most important thing there is so far as the long-term credibility of your work is concerned. We all hope for the video or picture or excerpt of our work that will go viral and become next week's Big Thing across the planet – this being the most publicised way that completely unknown people receive world-wide exposure – but the reality is that most such incidents occur with complete randomness; in any case, if your viral attempt doesn't include a cat in some manner, then you can pretty much forget it (which reminds me, I really must dig out some of those old photos of the tortoiseshell I had when I was growing up and think up a witty, anthropomorphising caption to add as she looks into the camera). For the vast majority of us, then, the route to establishing ourselves in the new world market of digital products is in getting our work reviewed and appreciated.

The political point of anything 'indie' is that it represents choice that isn't available via the mainstream. There's nothing inherently wrong with mainstream products, but it's important to remember that these items – purchased in their millions – are selected for you by a very small and – arguably – non-representative group of people. This small group of people effectively get to decide on what you will see and hear and read. Indie offers you an alternative.

Just as there's nothing inherently bad about mainstream products, however, there's nothing inherently good about independently produced ones. A self-published book could be brilliant, mediocre or – as my own unsatisfied reviewer declared – junk. The indie scene could be likened to a lucky dip in terms of quality – a vast, enormous, endless lucky dip as more and more people plunge into unregulated self-publishing of one sort or another – if it wasn't for the fact that the same medium which enables individuals to make their work available also enables other people to give an indication as to whether it's any good or not. The Internet is the medium which has liberated independent artists in terms of making their work accessible to an international audience; user feedback is the mediating mechanism which actually makes such a thing practical. But we have to use it for that to work.

These days, the line between mainstream and independent products is becoming increasingly blurred. When it comes to writing, self-publishing is still regarded by many with disdain, even though the written word was the very first unit of creation to be liberated by the Internet. Few people experience similar reservations when it comes to downloading Apps for their smartphones, however, many of which are the products of small companies or individuals developing from their bedrooms. We don't really care about the way in which an app was produced so long as we enjoy the end result and the ratings system is there to guide us in our purchase. But what we mustn't forget is that the very variety that's pushed as a selling point of smart phones – as immortalised by the slogan, "There's an App for that" – exists precisely because this market makes no distinction between products developed by large companies and those by bedroom programmers. Right from the start, the two have been treated exactly the same and as a matter of necessity: just think how slowly the smartphone market would have developed if only large companies were able to bring software to it.

Second Life, of course, is utterly dependent on independently produced products; there is no 'non-indie' industry to speak of in the metaverse – everything we wear and use and live in has been designed by a resident. Even the large clothing labels are usually just a single designer and a small collection of staff. One of the reasons that I refuse to fall out of love with SL is its implementation of a modern-day digital cottage industry, one which I see as a model for a much wider industry across the entire Internet. When the web first achieved mass take-up in the late nineties, people used to talk about the liberation it offered artists of all descriptions from the big industries of recording and publishing. Unsigned musicians could get their work out to a larger audience. Artists could get create virtual galleries. And writers could find a following for their work. There was an unspoken understanding that the huge riches awarded to the fortunate few that made it through the funnel under the old system were unlikely to be found by an enlarged group of active creators, but an honest living was never considered out of the question.

If only it were the case that consumers since then had started exploring the work of its lesser-known artists on a scale that changed the relationship society has with its culture; sadly, the main effect so far has just been to threaten the existence of big media through the illegal downloading of the very music and films they were pushing on us in the first place. Our imagination, so far, has failed us. But this isn't an opportunity that's about to expire on us and, in fairness, it takes a long time for old habits to be broken. Just like they said that the Internet would kill TV and it hasn't, we still seek – despite all the technological advances – to encounter our culture through 'trusted sources'. If we – the consumers – would really like to see this ultimately change, there are steps we can take right now about it.

One of those steps is to buy indie products from time to time. Often, they're more cheap than their mainstream equivalents. Sometimes – like 'AFK' – they're free. So it's hardly a great financial risk.

But – and I cannot stress this highly enough – after you've read or listened to or viewed it and if you liked the thing that you obtained, *leave a rating.* On Amazon.com, you only have to leave a 20 word comment in addition to your stars and, if that's really asking too much, you can just click on the 'like' button for that book instead. If you want independent producers to grow, do this to support them.

If you're a person who's bought or downloaded things and not left feedback and are feeling now that my whining is nothing more than a guilt trip, I'll come clean on something: I am just like you. I don't think I've ever left feedback on anything I've ever bought from the SL Marketplace. The truth is, it took a negative comment on my book to make me realise my own lack of support for others. I will be doing something about this in 2013: my new year's resolution is to leave feedback on things I enjoy as often as I can, even if it's just a twenty word statement; even if it's just to click a 'like' button.

I encourage you to join me.

22

The Evolution of Identity

First published February 2013, AVENUE Magazine

Recently on my blog I published a short extract from the new novel I've been working on, 'AFK, Again'. In the extract, Second Life private investigator Definitely Thursday reflects on the various categories of avatar profile she's encountered over the years, these including the Empty Profile (EP), the Aggressive Profile (AP), the Somebody Else's Quotations Profile (SEQP), the In Love Profile (ILP), the Promotional Profile (PP) and still more. For example:

> *"The Poetry Profile (PoP) attempts to map out the personality of the resident in picks via a selection of poems; subsets of this category are the Rhyming Poetry Profile (RPoP) and the Own Poetry Profile (OPoP)."*

My own profile's a mixture of promotional picks (please visit my website, please buy my books; that sort of thing) and references to a few significant SL friendships. It's pretty static – I rarely update it – and it contains, I have to admit, a quotation from somebody else – Stephen Fry, who once wrote, "You have no idea where I am as I do this, and I have no idea who, where or what you are as you continue to read. We are connected by a filament of language that stretches from somewhere inside my brain to somewhere inside yours." He was referring to the relationship he had as a writer to his readers, which is why I personally have selected it, but I also think it's a beautiful summary for the way we conduct our textual interactions in the metaverse.

Perhaps it seems like stating the bleeding obvious to say that our lives are becoming increasingly digital, but I don't think society as a whole has yet grasped the larger ramifications of this. As the media gets itself all tied up in debates over privacy and the real life social cost of excessive amounts of time spent online, the issue of digital identity seems to have gone largely unexamined. The elderly throw their arms up in despair at the sheer ridiculousness of it all; the middle aged embrace it, but at the 'bolt-on' level where online interaction is an occasional additional social layer; the young, meanwhile, are living it: to them, the online world is increasingly interwoven with the offline world and where the one meets the other is becoming more and more blurred. I'm generalising, of course. And I'm certainly not suggesting that the young have got it right. I belong to the middle category and, whilst I'm undeniably just a little bit in love with some of the possibilities that online interaction offers, I'm also mindful that human beings have evolved to be with other human beings *physically*: it's in our nature; it's primal; it's how we're meant to be. The thing is, social trends are entities in their own right and pay little attention to such socio-biological truths. And, barring some big, unforeseen event that sends everyone fleeing from their computers in terror, we are now a long way past the point of no return to a non-digital way of existence. One could, of course, argue that our mission must be to escape the limitations imposed on us by evolution and biology, and that digital identity is one such escape route.

Evolution is fickle beast, full of apparent contradiction. It's left us with predispositions and mechanisms that are both helpful and unhelpful in our modern age. On the one hand, we've evolved to live in groups and therefore survival of the fittest group has perhaps been a more important shaping factor to our genes than survival of the fittest individual over recent millennia. We know, for example, that hostility is a trait that leads to an increased risk of heart attack and it's been suggested by means of an explanation for this that hostile people would have had a corrosive effect on hunter-gatherer tribe strength such that their death would ultimately be beneficial. We know that women tend to live longer than men, perhaps because their ability to care for the young in a tribe – ie, to continue to contribute – outlasted a man's ability to hunt. There is also an emerging school of thought that a having different types of thinkers in your tribe would have been advantageous. The people we today diagnose as having ADHD could back then have been thought of as the fast hunter learners who acquired new skills simply through doing them. The people we today diagnose as having Asperger Syndrome could back then have been thought of as the thinkers who found new solutions to problems. As Temple Grandin once said, "Who do you think made the first stone spear? That wasn't the yakkity yaks sitting around the campfire. It was some Asperger sitting in the back of a cave figuring out how to chip rocks into spearheads." Strength through diversity isn't just a political correctness banner, it's evolutionary fact.

On the other hand, tribal life meant competition and aggression from other tribes. This has left us with a strong fear of the unfamiliar, a desire to protect our status quo and a desperate need to strengthen our position within a group for fear it will reject us and leave us at the mercy of others. It's possible that virtually all forms of prejudice and discrimination arise from this biological predisposition programmed into us by evolution. We make racist jokes because we have no connection with the targeted ethnicity – their 'not-us-ness' scare us – and because we hope we'll get a laugh from the people we tell them too, making them better friends and less likely to exclude us.

It could be argued that the greatest contradiction of the evolved brain, however, is that it's infinitely more complicated than perhaps it really needs to be, at least so far as survival within a tribe is concerned. Perhaps the original advantage brought about by its key distinguishing property – consciousness; awareness of self – is that it enabled us to step outside of our bodies mentally and, through this, gain a better understanding of the wider world around us: crucial for solving problems that require more than just instinctive knowledge. Out of this ability, however, came a whole set of other skills and properties, such as that of empathy, aesthetic appreciation and sense of identity. The more we've become conscious of social variation around us, the more we've sought to determine our own place within it.

In SL, the two places where we can give a first glance, 'snapshot' sense of our identity to others is through our avatar appearance and our profile. As I indicated earlier, the degree to which we use our profile as an identity tool varies from person to person and our individual usage also varies over time. The same could pretty much be said of avatar appearance. Huck has worn the same black shirt and jeans for the best part of a year, I'm afraid, but you shouldn't infer from this that my avatar appearance is unimportant to me. In fact, I do have a range of outfits and when I'm inworld for more than a few days in a row I do attempt to rotate them. But all of my outfits still say pretty much the same thing about me: that I'm a quiet, unassuming guy. My shape says the same thing. Way back when the default male shape in SL seemed to be a cross between a Greek God of War and an American Football player, I basically wanted a skinnier, frankly weedier looking avatar. Years spent in real life not able or wanting to fit in with any sort of stereotypical alpha male behaviour has left me enthusiastic to express a more gentle, more intellectual maleness. I've had a few AOs over the years too, but I've always eschewed anything with any sort of threatening stand. My current AO is something of a fidget, always stretching and moving from foot to foot. It makes me look a little uneasy when I'm amongst a crowd of solid or graceful standers, which is fine by me because that's exactly how I do feel amongst gatherings of people.

This said, however, it would be untrue to claim that these aspects of my identity are my *sole* identity. As I wrote in my very first column for AVENUE, the whole beauty of SL and its anonymity is that it allows us to explore aspects of ourselves which we might not have had the courage to explore in real life. There is nothing preventing us from exploring more than one of these. We can do these in our existing avatars to a certain extent, however the same anonymity which facilitates the first online identity can also facilitate the second and the third and the fourth.

I might decide to adopt a whole new writing style and persona, for example, spend time exaggerating my more eccentric qualities or live life as a female. For a while in 2011, I contemplated living as a pine cube with a gender-neutral name, just to see how people responded to someone where they had no cues whatsoever as to RL gender or lifestyle. One of the first things you discover in a new identity, after all, is that people respond to you completely differently. Identity is a socially constructed phenomenon. It's a two-way thing.

There are plenty of dark sides to this fragmentation of identity, such as exploring the freedom to express hate views, deliberate deception or anonymous bullying – all topics I have written about in various ways over the years. This is by no means by default a peaceful human voyage that lies ahead of us. Like it or not, however, digital identity is going to come the big issue of the decades to come and it's going to be a lot more complicated than sorting profiles into arbitrary categories. We need to start getting our heads around this issue and soon.

23

Second Life Updates

First published March 2013, AVENUE Magazine

In the days when I was new to the metaverse, it was unusual for a week to go by without some sort of blog update from Linden on the Second Life home page. In recent times, this frequency of communication seems to have dropped considerably. There were just nine posts made in the whole of 2012. Without wanting to sound like I'm jumping on the The End Is Nigh bandwagon, it is tempting to ascribe this to the general decay of SL commented on in so many places these days. It is, after all, a decay that can be seen in many places. Last week, I flew down from my skybox and took a look around some of the mainland sims surrounding the region I've lived in since 2007 and was staggered at the amount of abandoned land I found. It was like walking across a wasteland: parched, undulating ground stretching off in all directions, almost as far as I could see. All it needed was a piece of tumbleweed bouncing past or a post-apocalyptic, skeletal hand reaching out of the burned soil towards the scorched, tear-stained sky.

But wait. 2013 seems to have got off to a much more talkative start, with seven posts made in January alone. Does this denote a new direction for Linden's communications policy? As we enter the final six months leading up to SL's tenth birthday and the potential associated media attention, is Linden stepping up its Be Friendly Towards Residents campaign? My curiosity piqued, I decided to take a look at what topics our governors have deemed fit for discussion with us.

The first was the announcement that SL is now available to purchase as a product from amazon.com. Yes. It's listed under the 'Video Games' section of the website, in fact (and let's not get into the 'it's not a game' debate right now; no matter how right you are, the people you're making the point to will always regard anything that moves on a computer screen and isn't a video of an amusing cat on YouTube as a game; in any case, there isn't a section at Amazon for 'Metaverses and Virtual Worlds' so where do you suggest they put it? 'Patio, Lawn & Garden'?). As well as the basic free download, you can also acquire various inventory 'packs' for sums of actual money. The 'Premium Vehicle Pack' bundles a sailing boat, a dune buggy and a hoverboard with L$4,000 for the real world price of $24.95, whilst the 'Deluxe Vehicle Pack', retailing at $14.95, contains only the hoverboard, sailing boat and L$2,000. I suppose the best way to think about these things is as SL gift vouchers, only ones which cost more than the value of the cash they come with and which have thrown in a couple of novelty items you might use if you're a newbie for as long as it takes you to discover the experience of crossing a sim border.

Speaking as someone who's neither seen nor stepped upon a hoverboard in SL, I'm struggling to accept this as the hitherto undiscovered hook that's going to reel in metaverse newcomers by the million, yet the 'Starter Vehicle Pack' ($9.95) contains just this item and a mere L$1,000. Yes: out of all three vehicles created for this stunning new marketing tool, the one that Linden thinks people are most likely to buy by itself is the one that doesn't actually exist in the real world, which can't take any passengers, which is difficult to see and aesthetically appreciate when it's being used and – let's be honest – which is most likely to annoy other people. What's more, the 'Hoverboard Bonus Pack' contains *only* hoverboard extras – no lindens whatsoever – and costs $12.95! I rarely use exclamation marks in non-fiction, but this surely merits a minimum of three (you should be respecting me for my restraint). But if you think I'm against the idea of Amazon SL packs then you're wrong. In fact, I intend to dedicate next month's column to an analysis of the virtual bundles we might actually find enticing.

Returning to the list of Linden January blog posts, two of these concern the all-new 'Quicktips' video tutorials prepared by Linden for newbies. The first is a one minute introduction to avatar appearance, the second a guide to buying and unpacking items. Naturally, the latter cannot possibly fit into a minute and spends instead a second under three trying to make the various caveats to SL shopping (items bought should appear in your received items folder… except they might come in a box… and boxes need to be rezzed on land to be unpacked… oh, but not all land can be rezzed on… you need a sandbox (no explanation is given as to what a sandbox is)… click on the box to unpack it… oh wait, some boxes don't unpack automatically…) sound easy. All credit to the narrator – who sounds suspiciously like Torley Linden – for resisting the urge to scream hysterically, *Why are sellers STILL packing items into boxes and not even providing land to unpack them on?* Then again, it does rather sound like he's reading from a pre-prepared script, possibly with a gun to his head.

Another of the blog posts concerns interesting developments in the SL use of the Leap Motion controller, an as yet to be released controller device that reads real life movement in a manner presumably not all that different from Microsoft's Xbox Kinect. A video clip embedded in the post demonstrates the use of the device to control with hand movements the movement of an avatar, the positioning and sizing of objects (because we're all still building stuff out of prims), and the activation of gestures. Regular readers of my column will know I see a healthy future for real life movement metaverse interface; at the same time, anything which makes it any easier for people to unleash those twenty-something lines of ASCII spam across my screen or pre-recorded, not-even-funny-in-the-context-of-the-original-movie sound clips must carry with it the threat of the death penalty. So be warned, developers. Be warned.

Last of all, Linden's started posting on its blog highlights from its Destination Guide – a handful of destinations per blog post with a picture and a paragraph each to whet your exploration appetite. The most recent of these was themed around new art installations. It's been a while since I looked at some SL art and I was in the mood for something to cheer me up from the wastelands below my skybox, so I picked a couple of these – Citysphere and Bryn Oh's sim-sized 'Imogen and the Pigeons' and jumped into the teleport.

Citysphere is a large sphere covered in skyscrapers that you can walk around as though it's a small planet; sort of an SL ecumenopolis that – apparently – gets three times the land space of a sim onto its surface area, although the buildings have no actual function. Sticking to the ground as you walk around the miniature Trantor is achieved by means of a special sit script that enables you to walk normally whilst everything slowly turns upside down. It's more than a little disorientating to see your avatar dangling from the ceiling – by which I mean ground – and I couldn't decide whether a reorientation script hadn't been included a) because the artist didn't know how to write one or b) because however irritating, dizzying and nauseating it might have been, the effect is a powerful reminder that we're all of us upside-down to somebody. I'm guessing now probably (b). It is art, after all.

And then there's 'Imogen and the Pigeons', which deposits the arriving visitor in a wasteland not entirely dissimilar to my local SL neighbourhood, except with added cooling towers. Wound around one of them, a thin spiral staircase (watch your step, there's no railing) is one route up to the hundred metre high entrance to the main exhibit; a set of fallen blocks that arrange themselves into a staircase as you step on them (but turn the wrong way and they all fall back to the ground) is a second; a whirly chair for the can't-be-arsed-with-precision-movement avatars like yours truly is a third and if you're *really* lazy there's a teleport ball in the middle cooling tower that'll take you straight there. Thus, you arrive at the reception to the Therapist's office, one of many narrative signs informing you: *An unfortunate space / that the printers missed, / changed the psychologist's plaque / to read "The rapist" / Sadly the mistake / was not far from true, / as the therapist had / destroyed a mind or two.* That sort of therapist, then. In the office, we discover him examining his dead butterfly collection, each insect labelled with the name of one of his patients, except the butterfly for Imogen is missing. *He was the type of man / who felt he saw much clearer / from the darkened side / of a one-way mirror.* A few locations later, we find Imogen in bed in her room in the hospital and gazing out of the window at her free friends, the pigeons, gathered together on the telephone wire. On the sill, Imogen's still alive butterfly flaps its wings in a glass jar and clicking this takes you to an online video clip of Bryn releasing a newly metamorphosed butterfly into the sky. 'Imogen and the Pigeons' is absolutely packed with puzzles and detail that I couldn't even begin to describe here. What began as an intended five minute excursion ended up as a full hour exploring the various nooks and crannies of this enormous exhibit, and even then I left feeling I'd only scratched the surface. You could very easily spend a whole day exploring it. It is immense.

I'm glad that Linden appear to have decided we're worth talking to again. 'Imogen and the Pigeons' was also the perfect antidote to all that nothingness now surrounding my home and the vague worry that SL has lost its ability to move and inspire me. Of course, the plus side of being surrounded by wasteland where I live is I could have a lot of fun racing around down there in some sort of buggy. Aha. Suddenly, the Amazon Premium Vehicle pack makes sense…

24

And You're Done

First published April 2013, AVENUE Magazine

Last month, I examined in passing the Starter, Deluxe and Premium Second Life 'Vehicle packs' available from Amazon, which bundle Linden dollars with up to three featured vehicles, these being a hoverboard, a dune buggy and a sailing boat. Enthusiasts of any of these virtual pursuits will, I hope, forgive me for the somewhat sarcastic treatment of these products I gave. In the interests of transparency, it should be noted that the only one of these things I've ever tried is sailing, and that was only the once, and that was with someone I barely knew so that when I got ejected at a sim crossing and my avatar sunk to the bottom of the ocean like so much unwanted cargo I decided to fake my death and swim away, pretending I'd been lost at sea. Shhhh: don't tell her I'm still alive.

Try as I might, I just can't get all that enthusiastic about vehicles in SL. To me, it's all just a little too suggestive of that old SL-marketing-itself-as-a-video-game thing. I've never really been all that bothered by video games – more than ten minutes on pretty much any title and I'm bored by the sameness of it all; if I really wanted to battle my way through hoards of aggressive people, I'd visit my local Poundland. And isn't it safe to say anyway that people who actually do measure life enjoyment by time spent playing car racing games on other systems are unlikely to be all that impressed by anything SL can offer up in the genre?

This said, I suppose sailing is as much a social environment as it is a Driving Something Around thing, and I'm prepared to accept that my one experience wasn't broadly representative of the best that the occupation has to offer. Nonetheless, I still think SL can do better when it comes to marketing itself with the world's number one retailer. Here, then, are a few of my suggestions for alternate 'packs' to attract newbies and veterans alike.

Starter, Deluxe and Premium Cybersex Packs. Be honest, it's probably the first thing you thought of too, so let's get it out of the way. And, whatever your views on sex in the metaverse are, anything that contributes to the extinction of the 'freenis' (as a physical item, as a concept and as a word) has got to be a good thing. The Starter Pack, then – available in male and female variants, naturally – would come with medium quality genitalia plus a notecard with example emotes. Yes, this is going to encourage cutting and pasting, but let's be honest here: for anyone who needs to do this it will probably still represent a step up in quality. The Deluxe Pack would feature high quality genitalia plus a sex bed. The Premium Pack would feature the same plus a skybox fitted additionally with a sex-enabled fridge and hat stand. All genitals, incidentally, would contain a non-removable script that drops a large, horseshoe magnet on the head of the user if ever they should use the letter 'U' in place of the word 'you'.

Starter, Deluxe and Premium BDSM Packs. As above, but including various mechanical apparatus and collars, plus a copy of 'Fifty Shades of Grey' (a nice crossover with the more traditional Amazon product line), just to annoy the purists. The skybox would come with a dungeon. Alternatively, the fridge could be fitted with handcuffs.

Film and TV Tie-in Vehicle Pack Range. I'm not abandoning the vehicle pack concept entirely. All Linden has to do is substitute their vehicles with *exciting* vehicles. The original series Batmobile would be an immediate buy for me. KITT from Knight Rider. Airwolf. The James Bond Lotus Esprit that converts into a submarine. Thunderbirds. But there's more. The beauty of SL is not only that you can have the machines we know and love (the 'we' in most cases admittedly being men) but also the places they're associated with. Linden could commission licensed sim builds and then rent them out by the hour, and the packs would then come with vouchers for time bundled with the vehicles. Batmobile owners, then, could play in the Batcave; Airwolf pilots could rise from that hollowed out mountain; Thunderbirds fans could take off from Tracy Island; KITT motorists could drive their Knight Two Thousand into the back of a big black truck that drives endlessly round and round a bit of desert somewhere. And so on.

Personal Shopper voucher pack. If, like me, your ideal shopping trip to buy – say – a suit consists of a no-more-than-five-minutes visit to the MarketPlace that involves a quick search on 'Mesh suit' and the purchase of anything that looks half good within the first two pages of results, then you're probably missing out on many of the more sophisticated designs that SL has to offer. It never ceases to amaze me the near encyclopaedic knowledge of the latest SL fashions that many of the people I meet seem to be in possession of (and here – yes – 'people' can be read to mean in most cases women); that anyone can tolerate more than thirty seconds of a hair fair is a fact I hold in equal awe to such phenomena as quantum physics and the evolution of the human eye. So why not monetise this expertise by creating an elite team of personal shoppers who can take the newbie/uncaring avatar and guide/force/ruthlessly bully them through a shopping experience that meets their needs? I'm aware, of course, that there are people out there who do already offer this sort of service (my own avatar looked like something out of a black and white gangster movie – unintentionally, I might add; the look I was actually aiming for was 'intellectual' – until a very kind friend in 2008 diplomatically answered my enquiry as to what parts of my appearance she thought could be improved on with "all of them"); the difficulty is finding one when you actually need one and then knowing if they're actually any good. At least one of the so called experts whose profiles I've nosed within the last year was still wearing flexi hair: even I know that anything which disappears into your breasts is no longer considered the cutting edge. I propose, therefore, that the AVENUE editorial staff set the questions on the entrance exam for people wanting to become personal shoppers.

Novelty Weapons Packs. A fond memory of my time attending the weekly Writers' Circle event on Wednesday evenings at Cookie, then jointly hosted by Jilly Kid and Hastings Bournemouth, is of firing copies of the bible at Hastings with a bible gun that someone had passed to me and him returning fire with copies of Richard Dawkins' 'The God Delusion'. Possibly, you had to be there. Rarely do us peace-loving SL residents have a need for metaverse weaponry, but from time to time there comes along a moment when appropriately ironic armament can add just the right amount of situational comedy. Categories of weapon could include 'Amusing Projectiles That Aren't Penises', 'Griefer Seekers', 'Flower Power' (including the depleted uranium tipped 45 millimetre daisy shooter) and 'NRA support', the latter being there to ease the transition from real to virtual fire-arms when finally the US gets real about its batshit insane gun laws.

And finally, also on the subject of withdrawl support: *Virtual Smoking Pack.* In the UK, a debate is starting up over whether or not the smoking of electronic cigarettes should be banned in public places. Should the anti-smoking campaigners find success with their side of this argument, SL will become one of the last remaining places for Britishers to do anything that looks vaguely like smoking in front of other people. Linden should capitalise on this whilst it lasts (for, surely, it will not) with a product line of own-brand smokes (I have dibs on the 'Hax' brand, mainly because I like the idea of someone ordering "Two packs of Hax" at the cigarette counter), promoted through a campaign of banner and side bar advertisements: "You're never alone with a Lucky Linden"; that sort of thing. Smoking packs could also come with collectible cards featuring notable residents from the world of SL, such as artists, builders, photographers, griefers and poets (I'm available for pictures for this last category). They could also include smoke ring HUD attachments which give the customer control over a variety of novelty smoke sculptures to create with their virtual breath and lips. As an additional bonus, cigarette buyers who also own the Premium Cybersex Pack could be given the option to buy a limited edition phallic imagery smoke ring pack that sends a smoke train through a smoke tunnel: perfect, both for suggestive flirtation at parties and for the post-coital shared virtual cigarette

25

Second Life is Ten

First published May 2013, AVENUE Magazine

In June 2003, smartphones and tablet computers had not yet been invented. Windows XP was the dominant operating system and the idea that anything could possibly come along to challenge that was, frankly, laughable (Microsoft are still laughing at the very notion ten years later, only in a more hysterical manner). Facebook was a full half year away and Twitter not yet even a twinkling in its creator's eye. iTunes hadn't yet been released for the PC. VHS cassettes could still be bought in shops. *Finding Nemo* was educating movie-goers on the important issue of the anthropomorphism of fish and Beyoncé Knowles was topping the pop charts with 'Crazy in Love'.

And Second Life started.

Ok, so technically it started before that, depending on where you set your marker: October 2002, if you start counting from the opening of the public beta; March 2002 if you stand by the date that the first resident, Steller Sunshine (now over eleven years old), joined the private beta. Incidentally, Stellar's giant beanstalk – her first SL creation – can still be found at http://slurl.com/secondlife/Welsh/24/79/21 if you fancy a bit of metaverse archaeology.

But June 2003 is the date that Linden have set as SL's birthday, which means that SL is officially ten years old next month. No mean feat at all for a software product. It's come a long way during that time and many aspects of it must now appear almost unrecognisable to those very first residents, who had no mesh (not even sculpties), no voice, no windlight, no monetary system and no ability to teleport. That's right: SL in its first official incarnation had no teleporting, and when it was introduced it was only through a hub to hub system, where you had to make your own way across regions to and from the nearest teleport station.

In ten years, we've seen SL grow into a major phenomenon, talked about by the media and attracting large numbers of registrations every day, only to dwindle slowly into the (hopefully temporary) internet obscurity of continuing but no longer fashionable services. We've seen RL businesses and universities leap head first into the metaverse, only to depart within a couple of years, the promised potential of 3D Internet apparently unfulfilled. And we've seen Linden itself turn from an energetic company focused on education, open communication and user creativity into a much more opaque organisation seemingly concerned mainly with the commercial markets available to it and a more heavy-handed regulation of the metaverse (though not always without good reason).

But, despite all this change and turbulence, is the essence of SL now really so different from how it was back then? I say that it's not. Whilst there have been many technical improvements over the years, most of us still communicate primarily in text and the graphics upgrades have probably only served to enhance rather than create the sense of immersion we feel in the metaverse. RL businesses opening up in SL – for example, car manufacturers offering prim versions of their latest RL hatchbacks (let's be honest here, the proper word for this was 'advertising') – always was a red herring of no real consequence to the vast majority of residents; probably few of us even realised that they'd left until we read about it in a doomsayer blog post somewhere. And, whilst the 'feel from above' has undeniably cooled from the jollier days during such years as 2006 and 2007, I just can't believe that the average resident's level of affection for Linden is so significant to their day-to-day enjoyment of the metaverse that they consider the whole thing qualitatively ruined now. For sure, we all grumble about lag and sim crashes, but I've yet to hear anyone tell me they're leaving SL because they just can't handle the failed teleports any more. If anything, the day-to-day technical issues of SL have just taught us to be tolerant. No-one ever seems to mind when we disappear halfway through a conversation because we've all had exactly the same experience at some point or another. And, at the end of the day, SL crashing is pretty far down on the list of the worst things that can happen to you in life – second or otherwise.

When I first entered SL (in 2006), it was mainly as a work-avoidance strategy. I will admit also to having been curious about how any sort of online world could be quite so engrossing that people would spend anything like the hours in them I'd heard reported, but it was hardly a curiosity that required urgent and immediate sating – until the task of writing my first novel in ten years came along, that is. It was with a fairly sceptical mind-set, then, that I first came to the metaverse, not expecting it in any way to exceed my somewhat limited expectations. And, to begin with, it didn't even meet them. I had imagined that, at the very least, SL would be as smooth and as visually stunning as some of the first person computer games I'd seen advertised, and that this was presumably how it had achieved its following. I didn't think for one moment that my avatar would look quite so primitive as it did and that everything would be quite so, well, jerky.

In those days, initial orientation took place at Orientation Island and further help was then available at Help Island. As visually unimpressive as those places were, things did at least work there as they'd been designed to (it helped that numbers per island were restricted and that no-one in either of those places had yet had opportunity to learn about or acquire wearable scripted things). But then I discovered the mainland and got my very first introduction to lag. The region I got sent to was massively overcrowded and my avatar seemed to be unable to do anything other than walk on the spot. Also, the screen seemed to be spewing text endlessly from local chat and I had no idea how one was supposed to keep up with it (in those innocent first few SL days I imagined myself to be a great deal more noticeable than I actually was, and believed that somewhere in that soup of text was at least a line or two addressed to me). Within about five minutes, I experienced my first viewer crash. The whole thing was hopelessly confusing and I persisted only because I still thought there had to be something to this that I was missing.

It's hard now to remember the exact 'moment of immersion'. Making my first SL friend was certainly a big part of that. Learning the basics of building was another. The deeper and deeper I got, the more and more it felt like I'd discovered a whole new dimension to life that had previously been hiding in the shadows. SL started to change the way I thought about RL, but the way in which this was true was itself something that changed over time. Imagine a Venn diagram with two circles, one labelled 'RL' and the other 'SL'. When sceptics like I was first enter the metaverse, the two circles are completely separate: what could there possibly be in a 'computer game' that is of relevance to the real world? Then the two circles touch. Then they start to overlap. Finally 'SL' is just a smaller circle inside an enlarged 'RL', and the 'S' and 'R' prefixes are increasingly meaningless. There is only 'Life'; there is only that which is experienced, be it physical or virtual or otherwise.

Because all experience is ultimately *mental* experience. The first things we learn from SL might be how to use the interface and then how to make things happen in the shared creative space (as Linden now view it), but what we go on to learn can end up touching upon some of the most fundamental issues concerning human experience. How do we think about and identify with ourselves? How do we connect with others? What constitutes a place? What constitutes engagement in meaningful activity? The personal growth that SL offers us in these areas is applicable to our whole lives, not just our virtual ones. To give just a small and (literally) concrete example, creating buildings in SL has motivated me to study post-war architecture, which has enhanced enormously my enjoyment of building design in the physical world. Appreciation of that which we already have surrounding us is much touted these days as a key to long-lasting happiness: how ironic that one route to improving this should be through a virtual world where it's possible to create and explore the things you *don't* already have.

Happy birthday, Second Life. You started something amazing. Here's to the next ten years of metaversing.

26

Absent

First published June 2013, huckleberryhax.blogspot.com

To coincide with Second Life's tenth birthday, I thought I'd put down a few reflections on my own SL, focusing on some of the things that are no longer present.

Absent friends

Dizi

'You never forget your first friend in Second Life' is a phrase I've heard used exactly zero times in SL, but I'm willing to bet that if I dropped it in to an appropriately philosophical conversation I'd receive nods of earnest agreement from all my fellow participants. Dizi was my first SL friend and I couldn't have asked, paid or emotionally blackmailed for anyone better. With a fine knack for intelligent, irreverent banter, a quick grasp for the technicalities of the metaverse and a wonderfully clear way of explaining things, Dizi was exactly the right catalyst for turning my vague meanderings in the virtual world into something with some sort of purpose. She taught me how to build, she taught me how to emote and – perhaps most importantly of all – she taught me the pleasure of a tango at Bogart's. She also bought me my first pair of decent shoes, which might be an odd thing to list in any context, but I mention it here because it illustrates so perfectly her nurturing manner, not to mention her eye for the aesthetically pleasing (especially when it came to shoes).

Dizi eventually moved on from SL and I miss her enormously, but we still keep in touch from time to time via email. I'm lucky to have known her during her time inworld and I count hers amongst the most important friendships I have ever formed.

medi

medi was introduced to me by Dizi and I can honestly say that I've never met a more actually laugh-out-loud person in SL. This incredibly intelligent and literate woman adopted a porcelain doll as her avatar and dressed it up in all manner of outrageous outfits – blue and white gingham being a particular favourite design. Her condemnations were hilarious. Her insights were profound. I will never forget a conversation we once had where she told me she can't avoid in RL looking at how light falls on objects; I can't forget it chiefly for the reason that I have never looked at light in quite the same way since.

medi was ardently against sharing any sort of RL details, taking the view that this tarnished the illusion created by SL. Voice communication in particular was absolutely out of the question. It wasn't that we used this in our trio anyway, but when I did one of my first ever readings in SL she turned up (to show support) but refused to turn her speakers on, saying that hearing my RL voice would ruin the voice she had allocated to me in her head.

medi announced one day that she was leaving SL and that was the last that either I or Dizi saw or heard of her. She didn't leave in anger or sadness, and I rather suspect that she left her announcement until the last minute in order to avoid any drawn-out goodbyes. Much as I miss her, I can't help but grudgingly admire the way she managed this exit. But then, medi was magnificent in every way.

Nancy

Nancy was my first reader. We met in rather embarrassing circumstances. At a dance club, I was browsing her profile and saw an entry in her picks for an SL comedy club. Fascinated by this idea, I immediately clicked on the teleport button only to discover that the club didn't yet actually exist and she'd created the pick in her own house. In and of itself, turning up unannounced in someone's house isn't a total toe-curler on the embarrassment scale, however what I'd failed to notice whilst reading her profile was that Nancy had left the club before me and was partway through an outfit change in the moment that I materialised in her bedroom.

Nancy, however, was a wonderfully friendly and laid back person, and a moment's worth of awkwardness soon dissolved completely once we got chatting – the subject of which quickly became the Second Life novel I was halfway through writing at the time. Perhaps because of my memorable entrance, she read AFK the moment it was finished and became the first person to give me positive feedback.

I wish now I'd spent more time with this kind, gentle, lovely person. Nancy and I would occasionally IM each other and chat, and after a while she started coming to the Blue Angel Poets' Dive on Sunday evenings for the open mic poetry sessions I regularly attended back then. It was on one of these Sundays that she told me she was going to be away from SL for a while for health reasons. It never occurred to me that these would be the last words we would exchange, and Nancy died just a couple of months later.

Absent activities

Camping

I don't really miss camping. I miss the *excitement* of camping, although camping, of course, was never in any way exciting. To this day, I still can't quite believe I actually did it; I still can't believe I voluntarily stood around doing absolutely nothing for hours at a time in return for three measly Lindens an hour, thrown at my shoeless feet with contempt by whatever management it was that was hoping my mere presence in the vicinity of his or her establishment would bring people with actual money and a desire to spend it. If camping wasn't bad enough, there was also queuing for camping: a wait of additional nothingness for a camping spot to become vacant, only this time you got paid *nothing*. And then there was the wait to get into a sim with good camping spots, because the sim itself was full to capacity from people a) camping and b) waiting to be camping. Nobody ever even spoke to each other whilst they were camping because they were so full of self-loathing at having sunk this low any exposure of personality just made the loss of dignity worse. You came, you sat, you kept your mouth shut and you avoided looking anyone in the eye.

What was exciting about camping was the thing you wanted to buy with the money you got from it. This was your First Big Second Life purchase. You'd done the rounds on the freebie shops, flirted with trying to create a more interesting body shape by manually tweaking the slider bars and experimented with different colours on the lump of plasticine on your head which Linden so optimistically referred to as 'hair'. Slowly, but surely, the realisation had dawned on you that your avatar looked shit. Slowly, but surely, you started to covet the costing-money things which would make it look better. I estimate that the average newbie back then spent no more than a fortnight doing camping, because by then the desire for costing-money things had overwhelmed the ability to delay gratification any longer (as delays go, earning money though camping was a pretty fucking long one). Out went the policy on not spending any real money on SL and in came the Lindens, freshly minted from the LindeX. Camping was exciting because it was one of the things that represented our transition from 'I find SL interesting' to 'I find SL absorbing'. Camping was when we got hooked.

Exploring

In the early days of my SL, exploring meant walking along a road and seeing where it took me. An inventory devoid of landmarks and a friends list empty of, well, people, it was pretty much the only strategy I had available to me. Through this approach I discovered my first SL art gallery and had there my first SL conversation with another avatar. There was a sense, back then, of SL unfolding around me and that I was in control of the pace at which it unfolded. I could explore one sim of an evening; I could explore two or three or four: it was up to me.

It wasn't that I was unaware of other distant places, nor that I was totally ignorant on how to get to them. Back then, before both adult venues and their advertisements were moved to their own continent, the newbie avatar had virtual billboards declaring pleasure beyond their hedonistic dreams practically crammed down their throats the moment they took a step outside of whatever info hub it was they'd been sent to. I was indeed curious about 'cybersex' as a newbie (chiefly because I thought it sounded ridiculous), but I wanted to discover such places by myself. The idea of hopping about the grid, from one random point to another, made SL seem less like a world – less like one big place – and more like a collection of 3D websites. I wanted it to be a world.

All of which begs the question, why do I no longer explore SL in this way? In part, I suppose it's because most of the really interesting stuff for me tends to be on private sims disconnected from the mainland; now that my concept of SL as a world is established, it doesn't really need protecting any more. But I suspect the main reason is pure laziness. I've established my places and my people. I've grown my avatar identity. Whilst I do from time to time still do new stuff, I'm generally 'settled' in my SL ways. Is this a good thing? Probably, it's not.

Performing

I made a 'stand' of sorts about 18 months ago. A newcomer to the poetry events I was attending had various racial hate statements in her profile. She was a perfectly nice person to talk to in chat before you realised what she had listed in her profile; she certainly never in my company brought any of these views into conversation. A friend of mine then discovered these profile picks and stopped attending any events this avatar was present at. She dismissed event hosts' views that banning avatars with hate speech in their picks was a restriction of their freedom of speech.

By coincidence, I attended in RL a couple of days later a talk given by a black UK celebrity about her life in the 60s in Britain. Her family was one that had moved to the UK in response to the drive back then to recruit migrant workers, and they arrived only to be discriminated against in virtually every aspect of their lives. She would go into a shop, for example, and the shopkeeper would refuse to acknowledge her, far less serve her. I felt ashamed at my willingness to find a reason to ignore this person's hate speech.

I decided that my friend was right, that if we're agreed that hate speech should not be tolerated – and it's not like there's much legal doubt over that – then profile text should be treated alongside public chat. If I perform in front of an audience knowing that one or more people there are displaying hate speech in their profiles like little placards they've sneaked in with them (and, let's be clear here, I'm not talking about statements such as 'Immigration to the UK is a problem', I'm talking about statements such as 'UK SHOULD BE WHITES ONLY') then I'm passively endorsing such comments. A very easy way to not do this is simply to withdraw my performance. Which is what I did.

And I've hardly performed since. And I miss it.

Absent places

The Greenies home

Stepping into the Greenies home six years ago was like stepping into an entirely new metaverse, one where everything basically didn't look like printed out pictures stuck to the sides of variously shaped cardboard cereal boxes. Next to today's mesh buildings and objects, I will grudgingly admit that this wonderful sim of a giant 1950s lounge-kitchen overrun by miniature Little Green Men probably wouldn't look quite so stunning as it did back then, but it would still measure up pretty well. This was pre-mesh, *pre-sculpty* technology; knowing what I know now about building today, there are still things about that place that I can't work out. How, for example, did they line up all those prims without the joins being visible? Even in firestorm now, with its extra decimal points for X, Y and Z location, this is still an operation that ends up making me want to punch myself repeatedly in the face. And the texturing – oh, the texturing. How did they do that Coca Cola flowing out of the tipped-over bottle? How?

If you never visited the Greenies sim, you have missed out on a treat. Starting under the floorboards and emerging from a mouse hole (later, the starting point was moved to one of the kitchen cupboards), your mission, as such, was to locate all the little green aliens in their various humorous locations around this scaled up house – which, in its 1950s decoration, was the very embodiment of the science fiction B-movie. You found them dizzy on the turntable, you found them in the kitchen drawer and driving a remote control car and down the back of a picture frame. You found one sitting on a vibrator. Enjoying it. The detail was staggering; the build quality exquisite. The atmosphere (in particular, the repeating black and white sci-fi clip on the TV if you had stream turned on) was extraordinary. The Greenies was a glimpse of the graphical future potential of the metaverse, one which we are now becoming acquainted with through mesh – and already starting to take for granted.

Sawtooth

I've lived in a skybox over the same spot of mainland now for nearly six years. For most people living in such circumstances, the flow of neighbours in and out of your region is fairly constant, as it was for me for the first six months or so. And then a lady called Lorene moved in and bought up what she could (nearly half of the sim) and turned it into Sawtooth Mountain Resort.

Sawtooth was a peaceful community of rented log cabins, with space allocated also for communal areas: a camp fire, a paddock with grazing horses, a small river, a greenhouse, a church and a pond. I was happy for my own land at ground level to be a part of this as an open space, since I'm not keen on living on the soil; my concrete brutalist building would have looked quite out of place down there and it was perfectly happy floating at 200 metres on its atomic motors (you do realise that's how skyboxes float, right?).

I got on with Lorene, but a year or so after she'd established Sawtooth, she decided SL was not for her and moved on. Perhaps she wanted to leave a return open to her, however, because she left Sawtooth in its entirely. For something like three years, the resort remained untouched, the cabins completely unoccupied. I used to drop down from time to time for a peaceful wander in what became over time in my head my secret personal relaxation zone.

Compared to modern mesh builds, there was nothing especially remarkable about the constructions in Sawtooth, but taken as a whole, the resort had a tranquil cohesiveness about it. Lorene eventually realised she wasn't coming back and, about a year or so ago, she got rid of the land. I'm back to the flow of neighbours in and out, now, but I'll always remember Sawtooth as something special.

Absent ideas

Business

When I joined SL, there was one big thing that it was renowned for and two that it wanted to be renowned for. The one big thing it was renowned for was sex, which Linden ended up moving onto its own continent and adult sims, causing huge controversy amongst residents at the time. For example, enormous helicopters came to airlift entire adult clubs across the sea – some still with dancers in them – resulting in three venues being lost at the bottom of the ocean in a series of "unrelated" in-flight accidents. Actually, it wasn't that controversial, but you'd have been forgiven for thinking so at the time.

The first of the two things it wanted to be renowned for was business, by which I mean RL companies establishing an SL presence. I'm still not entirely certain how it was that Linden actually visualised the manifestation of this idea. What exactly was there that a car company, for example, could achieve in the metaverse? Were they expected to bring products to the SL market such as officially licensed versions of their RL creations? Were they expected to promote their RL business through inworld sales reps and SL freebies? I'm fairly certain I must still have an old Mazda hatchback in my inventory from this period; thinking of it now brings back a fuzzy memory of a gleaming showroom in a pristine sim – spoiled only by newbies zooming and bumping around in their free Mazdas. I might be wrong, but I think it possible that a constant stream of simulated fatal road accidents just outside the store wasn't quite the image the company had been hoping for in the metaverse. It might not have been Mazda, by the way – there were quite a few car companies in SL back then.

Then again, the very same question – what were they expecting? – could probably have been asked of the web back in the days of its early expansion prior to the dotcom boom. Companies practically fell over each other back then to throw themselves onto that bandwagon, with little actual strategy as to what they were going to do on the web once they got there. Much the same could be said today for the continuing stampede of businesses to Facebook and Twitter. Does anyone actually follow these organisations for reasons other than a Like getting you some sort of discount voucher or extra levels in Angry Birds? Is there anything other than simple raw exposure to be gained from establishing your business there?

I've more or less come to the conclusion that simple raw exposure was about the only bit of the SL business boom that was actually worked out. In came organisations like Vodafone, Sony, Mazda, Renault, Mercedes, Coca Cola, the BBC and Calvin Klein, lured by Linden's seductive talk of SL as the '3D Internet'. The rhetoric was all about developing new ways of "interacting and developing our relationship with our customers", but really this was just another stampede of organisations wanting to be part of the Next Big Internet Thing. The details of what they were actually going to do could be worked out once they'd opened their nice shiny building with their logo on the front: basically, a website made 3D.

But Second Life didn't become the Next Big Internet Thing; once that was obvious, all the businesses left.

Education

The second of the two things SL wanted to be renowned for was education. There was a lot of talk about this back in 2007, with a number of universities signing up and establishing virtual presences, encouraged in part by the reduced tier Linden was offering at the time for educational organisations. I'm not unduly bothered by the departure of business, because I see that only as a consequence of SL's mainstream popularity: if SL were to become big one day, the businesses would return in the snapping of a finger; no-one's really the worse off for their absence and it's not like they attract new people to the metaverse. But the failure to establish SL as a worthwhile platform for learning is an enormous shame.

Unlike business, it's not hard at all to imagine how education could work in the metaverse. In the real world, training sessions are hampered by two key logistical and financial factors: venue and travel. For sure it's a swings and roundabouts situation: no-one would deny the benefit of being in the physical presence of a skilled trainer for a teaching session, but if that trainer happened to live on a different continent to you and attending a session run by him or her in Second Life would cost you $50 instead of the $1000 you simply couldn't afford on travel and accommodation, wouldn't that be an acceptable compromise?

Obviously, SL isn't the only way in which online education can be achieved. There's a staggering number of educational videos to be found on YouTube these days, from filmed speeches to custom made animations: many of these are excellent and I think it would be true to say that the earnest learner has never had it quite so good. But teaching has always held interaction close to its heart and this is the unique selling point that SL has – had – to offer online education. When you're in a class you get the opportunity to ask questions. The teacher gets to gauge from your questions your understanding and can modify his or her strategy. As an RL trainer myself from time to time, I often find myself branching off – pulling up completely different slides from those I'd originally intended to talk to – because a question from an attendee reveals something I need to explain better.

And learning, let's not forget, is a social experience. The conversations we have with our fellow learners help us to make sense of the material we're hearing. No YouTube video gives you the opportunity to whisper in the ear of classmates who are hearing the exact same thing as you are at the exact same moment.

Second Life is now marketed by Linden as a 'shared, creative space'. In one respect, that's fine: I'm certainly not going to undermine the value of creativity. But most of the education institutions have gone now: it's an opportunity missed and a lesson not learned.

Absent products

Mega prims

Oh how I cheered when the switch got flipped removing the ten metre limit on prim length (I think it was at about the same time that mesh got introduced). I didn't immediately optimise my skybox, but when I did I managed in the space of about an hour to reduce the prim count for the building shell by almost fifty per cent. More to the point, I was able to ditch every last mega prim I'd used in my previous optimisation. If I could have, I'd have lit a fucking great big fire and burned the lot of them in celebration.

Mega prims were a necessary evil if you wanted to build anything bigger than a garden shed and not have it suck dry the measly 117 prim allowance on your 512m plot. Imagine a shoe box with the lid taped on and one of the long sides cut out and you pretty much have the shape of my skybox. It measures now 32m by 16m and is 10m high. To do this in old, ten metre restricted prims would cost a staggering twenty prims; today, it can be done in two. Of course, to reduce this number, I originally built the skybox as 30m by 15m but that still cost me sixteen prims – and that's before I got to the windows, let alone the furnishings. With mega prims, I managed to reduce the sixteen to a very respectable five. But not without pain.

I don't understand how mega prims were made: through some sort of black SL art, I suspect, that involved naked dancing and incantations. Or possibly a viewer bug which talented residents exploited for the brief period that it existed (you decide which is most appealing). The thing with mega prims was that they only came in certain dimensions – dimensions which you couldn't adjust (because the moment you attempted to do so they snapped instantly back to the ten metre limit) and dimensions which very rarely coincided with the actual size of prim that you wanted. You only realised this, of course, after you'd trawled through the eye-bleedingly long list of mega prims in your inventory – twice, because you just couldn't bring yourself to accept that your perfectly reasonable dimension needs could not be met. Even the builder's HUD I later obtained ended up making me want to stab myself: although it conveniently took size requests from the command line and searched for something that matched, it didn't realise that a 15m x 30m x 0.5m prim was functionally the same as a 30m x 15m x 0.5m prim, making every ultimately unsuccessful search six commands long and a headache in trying to make sure you'd exhausted all the X, Y and Z combinations. I'm an ungrateful bastard, I know; mega prims ultimately saved me a great deal of land impact prior to the ten metre limit removal, but Christ they were a pain.

Of course, mega prims are still around today: the ten metre limit might have been removed, but a sixty-four metre limit was then imposed and mega prims exist at sizes up to sixty-four *thousand* metres (that's 256 whole sims lined up next to each other). Thankfully, since it's unlikely I'll ever be able to afford a land parcel that exceeds 64m in any direction, using these things again is a horror I will never have to contemplate.

Flexi Jackets

In much the same way that I kind of like the way 1980s programmers became increasingly ingenious at getting more and more from the old eight bit computers, I have a certain affection for the ways in which clothes designers overcame the limitations of the old 'painted-on' shirts and jackets prior to the introduction of mesh. As mesh continues its apparel assault, I imagine there must be designers now lamenting that their once clever tricks for adding hoods and collars and cuffs and rolled up sleeves and all manner of other bits in some way embellishing an avatar's upper body (a single jacket could have 30+ prims in its folder) will soon become about as relevant as Ray Harryhausen's amazing stop-motion modelling techniques are in the digital effects era. Unless they sell in InWorldz, of course…

Well, their day isn't over just yet. Lots of this clothing still gets worn today because the best of it still looks pretty good. I have a tuxedo, bought years ago from Blaze, that continues to look perfectly respectable. Amazingly, this doesn't even use that little prim flap to be found at the bottom of so many men's jackets of what I propose become known now as the paint-prim hybrid (PPH) era. The only prim garnish to be found on it anywhere is a little sculptie bow tie. Awww.

Any jacket that employs those strips of flexi-prims in order to give them a 'loose' feel, however, may now become extinct. Seriously; I really hope I never see another of these again. Similarly, any jacket with one of those wrap-around cone-shaped prims to give it a wide flare at the bottom has my permission to die. It looked great in the static picture you clicked on to buy it; as soon as you tried to move, however, it looked like you were wearing some sort of portable iron lung.

Nobody especially likes deleting inventory, so dump all of this stuff in a special 'retro' folder and intend to wear it again for laughs at the 2023 SL reunion. Of course, by then we'll all be wearing the rigged mesh version of 'Ruth' and commenting on how perfect the emulation is. Ah, the irony.

Absent addiction

In AFK I wrote about a character who was – by her own admission – addicted to Second Life. She spent as much time inworld as she possibly could; she even slept logged in so that the dingding of any IMs coming to her during the night would wake her up.

I can't say that I've ever been *that* addicted to SL, but for sure there was a long period – of several years – when any day without at least some metaverse time felt hopelessly incomplete. I'd even go so far as to say that I regarded SL time during these years as the period during which I could be most true to myself as I felt myself to be in my non-working hours. SL was where I existed, socially. To a certain extent, I had good reasons for that.

It was more than a little ironic that I should have felt that way about the metaverse, since one of my curiosities about it in the first place was the whole issue of online world addiction. The key reason that I entered when I did was as task avoidance from working on a book I was writing at the time, but that's not to say I didn't also have questions I wanted answering. One of those concerned addiction. I'd heard a few months earlier about a young man in Japan who had actually died from sitting in one place for too long whilst he was gaming in an online world. I just didn't see how that was possible.

Although I personally never fell victim to such a level of addiction as that, I came close enough that I could see clearly how it was possible. I remember a day fairly early on in my residency when the whole grid went down for several hours. This used to happen every now and again back then, but rarely for more than a few minutes. Linden posted a message on the SL website encouraging us to view this downtime as an opportunity to get reacquainted with our first lives again. "Go and walk your dog," they joked. I wanted to scream.

Interestingly, time spent on the internet has been proposed as a possible factor in the current downward trend in UK crime. The proposal is that young people who might previously have spent time getting up to anti-social shenanigans in the evening are now spending their free time online at home. There's no evidence for this as yet, far less any idea as to *what* on the internet might be most responsible, but the reduction in crime – and through a period of economic depression most commonly associated with an *increase* in crime – is marked and experts are scratching their heads in genuine bewilderment. There has to be something they hadn't thought of before and the table is open to all ideas.

Few people would complain about crime reducing, but what if the cost of that is internet addiction? As online, graphical environments such as that offered by SL become more and more immersive, will more and more people surrender their entire lives to the virtual world of their choice?

I'm no longer addicted to SL, but neither am I someone who has to leave it completely in order to be free of it. I go inworld sometimes as little as half an hour in a week. Occasionally, I get the desire to do a particular thing and can spend much longer, or visit every day for a while. But, somehow – and I'm not entirely sure how or why – the need to be in whenever I can is now just a distant memory. I'm perfectly content for SL to be just a thing I sometimes enjoy.

The metaverse still fascinates me; I follow news about it avidly and there are often things I read about which I decide I have to witness or try for myself. I still consider myself very much a resident. But SL has lost its hold on me. For the most part, I'm glad about that.

For the most part.

27

Living in your Gender, in SL

First published June 2013, AVENUE Magazine

A professional acquaintance of mine in RL recently transitioned from male to female identity. Involved as I have been only on the very periphery, this and a similar occurrence several years ago have both been very interesting events to reflect on. I am lucky to work in a tolerant, progressive organisation that prides itself on its self-perceived inclusivity. Hypothetical principles are all well and good when it comes to anti-discriminatory employment policy; when a concept stops becoming abstract and gets real, however, we discover all sorts of fine detail to conflict with our deeper, our less intellectual modes of being.

For example, an issue arose in the earlier of these two cases regarding use of the female toilets. A number of female employees who were okay in principle with the idea of – as they saw it – a man dressed as a woman doing office duties, voiced anger at this person being allowed to use their conveniences. What this illustrates is that 'tolerance' only goes so far when it comes to how people actually relate to someone going through a change in their identity. Interestingly, a recently-built high school near where I live did away with girls only, boys only, women only and men only toilets, opting instead for single toilet facilities with wide open entrances and cubicles with doors from ground to ceiling: a few people were similarly uncomfortable with this idea at first, but the end result of it is that toilet bullying – a long-standing problem in British schools – has been all but eradicated there. This new approach to gender division (or rather, lack of) has been accepted, ultimately, because people empathise with the idea of being bullied in out-of-sight, isolated places. We can adapt to significant changes when we are sufficiently motivated and when we are sufficiently personally connected to their rationale that they make sense.

About twenty years ago, my mother told me about a person in their early twenties who sat next to her on the train to work each morning. Having made the transition from male to female identity, this young woman wanted to talk to her about 'women stuff' like clothes and hair and make-up and shoes. A lot of her questions seemed at first to my mother to have a sort of clichéd superficiality about them – they were almost child-like in their complexity; the sort of questions, perhaps, a young girl might ask her mother. Although she 'played along' with the conversations, a part of her doubted the sincerity of the context. It felt incongruous. This was not, after all, a young person with learning difficulties. When we discussed this further, however, we realised that a recently transitioned female who'd spent most of her life being socialised as male would have few common points of cultural reference with women. Put simply, she'd had little experience of talking to women as a woman and needed a non-threatening, non-judgemental role model with whom she could learn some of these female socialisation 'basics' that life's conditioning so far had denied her.

Perhaps more importantly, she also just needed to have conversations with someone where she was spoken to as a female – and what better way to do this than through female topics of conversation? In thinking now about the issue of the colleague using the female toilets, I'm struck by how essential to acceptance female ritual must be to someone recently transitioned to female (or how essential male ritual must be to someone recently transitioned to male). The complainants might have defended their proposed restrictions to toilets access (none were ultimately made, thankfully) as some sort of limitation that ensured one person's 'preferences' didn't impose on others, not realising the fundamental importance of such ritual and not sensing that this issue of identity begins way deeper than the surface layer of clothing and hair style and make-up.

But perhaps most important of all is how this case demonstrates that the supposedly 'tolerant' co-workers revealed through this complaint that they weren't really thinking of this person as a female at all, but as a male, and thereby ultimately denying her her need to be spoken to as a woman for the sake of her own developing identity. To what extent is our identity influenced by that which others project upon us? Quite a bit, if you consider such theories as Henri Tajfel and John Turner's hugely influential 'Social Identity Theory' as valid.

But even if you try harder than these women did to empathise, it's still not easy to think about a person of one biology as the opposite gender when you're face-to-face in conversation with them, particularly if you knew him or her before they started their transition. Ultimately, it's the presence and absence of a hundred tiny little details which create the sense of incongruity we feel, much as we don't want to feel it, far less acknowledge it. We do our very best to take manual control and override all these automatic associations, but we have a lifetime of conditioning to overcome in those moments. The end result can often be that we come away worrying we haven't been natural with our friend or colleague and that they might have sensed our subtle disorientation – and we might be right. To a certain extent, there's not a great deal that can be done about this in the short term other than maintain our very best efforts to think of transitioned or transitioning friends as belonging to their chosen gender: eventually, the societal associations concerning gender will weaken and become rewritten, and perhaps future generations will consider our mental inflexibility absurd.

In the meantime, though, where can transgender people experience being treated and spoken to as – or, perhaps more importantly, *thought of* as belonging to – their chosen gender? Where can they explore their identity unencumbered by the baggage of others who are at worst overtly prejudiced and discriminatory and at best struggling to overcome their own institutionalised conditioning? The Internet in its widest sense has, to some extent, provided this medium for some time now: there was internet chat before the web and social networking now allows us to build whatever personal profile we desire. The metaverse, however, takes this to a whole new level of interaction. Second Life allows the anonymity that other forms of internet interaction provide, but it also allows us to adopt the visual appearance of our chosen gender and to exist in three dimensional spaces with others. As an opportunity to experience being treated by others in a chosen gender role on a day-to-day, moment-by-moment basis, it must be without historical precedent. Yes, it's a reduced sensory environment and communicating in text is not the same as spoken interaction, but it is at least an equal playing field with everyone else.

Concealment of biological gender does, of course, carry with it the uncomfortable issue of deception. If a transgender person exploring a female identity chooses not to make known her male biology inworld in order to experience properly being regarded as female, is she then guilty of deceiving what could potentially become very important friends in her life? Even though SL's terms and conditions are clear that no person is under any obligation to reveal their RL gender and that telling others the RL details of a resident – including their gender – is a serious breach, the perception continues that knowing such fundamental information about someone is some sort of human right. What we need to understand is that a transgender person is not 'pretending' to be the gender they adopt. They have always felt themselves to be this way, but that is not to say that they have had experience in living it. All too often, SL gets spoken of in the same breath as comments on sexual behaviour, with concealment of identity assumed to mean some sort of sexual misdemeanour; one of its most praiseworthy qualities, however, has to be the opportunity it gives people to *just be* in whatever way it is they want to be: through going shopping together, through irreverent chat, through looking at art together, through whatever.

And if a close SL friend should choose to reveal that they are transgender, we should look upon this as nothing less than a gift. For us, also, this is an opportunity. Those two hundred tiny details won't be anything like as apparent in metaverse interaction as they are in RL and our own sense of incongruity will be greatly reduced. As it does in so many other ways, SL helps us to experience something abstract as something plain and ordinary; the absence of detail allows us to see through that which might normally distract and to connect at that level where we are all of us just everyday people.

Perhaps it and the virtual worlds which will follow might even speed up in RL the weakening of our socially programmed associations. I, for one, won't miss them.

28

Linden's adventure products: dio and Versu

First published July 2013, AVENUE Magazine

Just over a year ago (February 2012), we discovered that Linden Lab had acquired experimental game studio Little Text People, a venture set up by Artificial Intelligence specialist Richard Evans and Interactive Fiction author Emily Short. The day after the purchase, Linden CEO Rod Humble left comments on the New World Notes blog which indicated the company was developing new products that had nothing to do with Second Life. Rumours had been circulating the previous year that Linden were interested in developing text adventures, although a tweet by Humble in September 2011 had appeared to deny this.

Twelve months later, Linden have launched first 'dio' (at the end of January) and then 'Versu' (in the middle of February), and we have not one but two new products based around the text adventure genre, the first a web-based platform and the second an iOS app. Neither are in any way related to SL, and if it wasn't for the banner ads for Versu recently added to the SL website, you could be forgiven for having completely failed to notice these new companions to our beloved digital world in its parent's product portfolio; nothing about these launches has so far (at the time of writing) been announced on the SL site. This does though add some possible light to the sudden flurry of posts since the start of the year in the 'Featured News' section of the SL dashboard: perhaps Linden are hoping new users of these two products might pay SL a visit and want their engagement with the community to appear a little more, well, in existence.

Dating back to 1975, text adventures started out as games where descriptions of locations were given in text and you were able to move around and do things by typing in simple instructions such as 'Go north' and 'Get sword' and 'Kill troll'. In the very first text adventure, for example ('Colossal Cave Adventure', written by Will Crowther), players were greeted with the following at the start of the game:

You are standing at the end of a road before a small brick building. Around you is a forest. A small stream flows out of the building and down a gully.

Typing, 'Go in' then gave this update:

You are inside a building, a well house for a large spring. There are some keys on the ground here. There is a shiny brass lamp nearby.

Games were eventually completed by using objects found such as the keys and the lamp to solve problems encountered. A darkened room, for example, might yield no secrets without that shiny brass lamp lit, but you might have to source oil and matches elsewhere before you could do that.

Text adventures were popular in the very early days of home computing, with titles such as the 1982 adaptation of Tolkien's *The Hobbit* achieving over a million sales in the UK. As the graphical capabilities of those machines developed, however, the more immediate appeal of arcade style games swiftly pushed adventures out of the mainstream market. But a small and dedicated community of writers and players remained loyal to the genre and new games have continued to be created ever since. Whilst they might be more difficult to get into initially than a game of Space Invaders, text adventures can be very immersive once you've got your head around them and the pleasure at solving a complex problem is immense.

Two key developments in adventures as the memory capacity of computers grew were the addition of pictures to location descriptions in some games (though these were still considered 'text adventures' since the medium of interaction remained text) and a greater focus on the quality of writing. The text descriptions in very early games were necessarily short and functional since anything more indulgent would have quickly filled up memory; as this ceased to be a limiting factor, however, more lengthy and literate narratives could be created. Over time, the term 'interactive fiction' became adopted to reflect this shift towards more immersive writing. Today, the term 'text adventure' is often used to refer to games where the focus is on solving puzzles and moving around an environment, and the term 'interactive fiction' used to refer to games where the focus is on narrative. This is a useful distinction for the exploration of Linden's new products, since dio would appear to be built around the text adventure approach and Versu is very much a platform for interactive fiction.

In fact, one of the first adventures to be found at dio (www.dio.com), which you access via the web and can log into using your Facebook account, is an implementation of none other than Will Crowther's Colossal Cave Adventure (www.dio.com/places/colossal-cave). The dio approach, however, does not require anything to be typed in: instead, the options available to you in any given location are arranged down the left hand side of the screen like the navigation buttons of a turn-of-the-century web page. The location text, pictures and messages display in a frame in the middle of the screen and there is space to the right of this for visitors to leave their comments. For me, the photographic illustrations instantly cheapened the feel of the Colossal Cave Adventure, but then text adventure enthusiasts always did argue that graphics ruined the visuals. Moreover, the arrangement of text and pictures on some of the dio titles feels a little 'scrapbook'. Still, it's early days. The first blogs were hardly works of art either.

But it's not just adventure games that can be created using dio. A text description of a place could be a real place or an historic place or a remembered place or a hypothetical place. A teacher could create a Victorian street of shops for pupils to explore. Distant relatives could create 'tourable' versions of their homes to show off. Holiday photos of places visited could be linked together as an album of pictures and jotted down memories. And so on. In a sense, dio kind of does for text adventures what SL did for first person shooter games: it takes a way of exploring an environment and broadens this beyond merely 'game'. dio 'places' are not just restricted to spatial environments either: suggestions made on the site for content include hobbies and interests, such as dios that show off any collections you might have (think places on a shelf). This, therefore, is Linden's 'Pinterest Product', a new way for linking pictures and text that challenges the dominance of the blog and Facebook format: items linked conceptually rather than chronologically. At a simplistic level, it could just be used as a website creation tool.

Versu (www.versu.com), on the other hand, is only a dedicated interactive fiction platform, the obvious outcome of the purchase of Little Text People. Currently only available as an app for Apple devices, the download comes with three free stories and a fourth available to purchase – all written by award winning interactive fiction writer Emily Short. No doubt, the range of titles for sale will grow over time, especially once users are able to generate their own content. Currently this isn't an option, although there are plans to introduce it in the future.

The Short stories are a collection of nineteenth century tales, the freebies consisting of 'An Introduction to Society', a Versu tutorial that follows schoolgirl Lucy taking instruction from her grandmama on how to behave in polite society, 'The Unwelcome Proposal', an adaption of Mr Collins' proposal to Elizabeth Bennet in Pride and Prejudice, and 'The House on the Cliff', a mystery story taking place on an apparently empty estate following a horse and carriage accident. On entering a story, the reader is given a choice of characters to play and narrative is presented from that person's perspective from that point onwards.

As with dio, there is no text input for the Versu stories and your options are made available via menus. Don't mistake this for a simple system, however: the options available are numerous. When Lucy takes tea with her grandmama, for example, these include stirring her tea, sipping it, slurping it, checking the level in the teapot, pouring out a cup for Grandmama, spilling a cup on Grandmama and many more besides. The response of other characters to your actions will depend upon a number of factors, including their personality, abilities and mood. And all of this complexity is gift-wrapped in Short's sumptuous narrative and accompanied by beautiful line art illustrations. Overall, they brilliantly showcase Versu as a reading experience and set a high standard for future authors to live up to. I hope there will be more titles available soon.

Blogoshpere comment on dio and Versu at the time of writing is sparse, since they are both still very recent releases. Some initial disappointment has been expressed that two products which appear at face value to do a similar thing are not compatible with each other. dio and Versu, however, are conceptually different things and targeted at different audiences. They both have immense potential as content platforms and of course both will succeed or fail depending on the content created for them. I used to write text adventures many years ago and I like both of these products. I have two new toys to play with, therefore, which take me back to a way of thinking about stories that I haven't entertained for a long time. That they both come from Linden – the company responsible for the product that has perhaps most engaged my imagination and creativity over the last ten years – is just the icing on the cake.

Update: dio and Versu were both dropped within a very short time of Rod Humble's departure from Linden and Ebbe Altberg taking up the reigns as CEO. Happily, an online campaign for Versu saw an effective reversal of this decision and the IF platform lives on.

29

Fatal Crosspost: Coming soon to a conversation near you

First published July 2013, AVENUE Magazine

Asimov once wrote of his pride in coining the word 'robotics', a term now commonly used to describe – and this can surely come as no surprise – anything pertaining to the technology or use of robots. It might seem odd that an author of literally hundreds of books should have ranked so highly the invention of a single word – one which, let's face it, would probably have made its way into our language in any case – in his audit of personal achievement; I'm totally with him on this, however. After nearly seven years of life in the metaverse and approximately half a million words committed in some shape or form to the subject, the marriage of just two of them delights me as one of my favourite creations: I invented the term 'fatal crosspost'.

'Fatal crosspost' might not be quite so universally obvious a term as 'robotics', however I'm relatively certain that most Second Life residents will understand its meaning without too much thought. It is, of course, the accidental typing of a comment into person X's instant message box instead of person Y's. Not just any comment. Let's be really clear here: simply typing any old innocuous thing into the wrong IM box by mistake is not what I'm talking about at all. That, of course, would be just a *benign* crosspost, the sort of thing we follow-up with "Wrong window; my apologies" and to which the crosspostee typically responds with a smiley face and a polite 'lol'. No. For a fatal crosspost to occur, the thing accidentally typed has to be monumentally one of the worst possible things you could say to that person in that moment. For example, a comment *about* person X meant for person Y. An uncomplimentary comment. As a general rule, it's unusual for me to make uncomplimentary comments about other people; one might think, therefore, that the law of averages alone would result in the number of benign crossposts made vastly outnumbering the number of fatal ones. This is not the case. In fact, I've found the benign crosspost to be a much less common occurrence than probability would predict based on the mental challenge posed by juggling two, three, even four IM conversations at once. On the other hand, those moments of immense peril involving immature conversations about someone nearby seem to attract the accidental crosspost like gravity attracts matter.

This is not to say that the benign crosspost can do no harm. Accidentally crossposting a comment on, say, the state of the economy into the IM box of someone you've intimated has your complete attention would be embarrassing for the crossposter and potentially humiliating for the crosspostee. Such a crosspost could indeed turn out in the long-term to be fatal. But the true fatal crosspost requires no time for its consequences to become apparent; its impact is as subtle as the kiss of a flying brick smashing into your face. And the torchlight embarrassment felt previously at an awkward crosspost will become in the sun-like glare of the sheer shame of an FC as minor as accidentally letting out in conversation one of those high-pitched sneezes you've always tried to repress in public. The fatal crosspost is the noisy fart you let out during your annual appraisal with the line manager you've always had a secret crush on by comparison.

I'm not quite sure why the creation of this phrase gives me so much pleasure. One theory I have is that the sheer mortification experienced at my own incidences of fatal crosspost is so intense I've disproportionately attached immense pride to the making of the phrase in order to convince myself that all the pain I've experienced and caused was in some way worth it in the end.

The mollified corpses left in my fumbling wake are the unfortunate collateral damage of genius, if you like: I might have seriously upset perfectly decent people with my social ineptitude, but without those subsequent moments of utter self-abhorrence I might never have achieved the greatness of inventing this amazing phrase. Incidentally, I'm not not mentioning here examples of my own personal FCs here out of consideration for the privacy of the crosspostees insulted by them, nor out of any attempt to reduce damage to whatever impression you might currently hold of me: the reason I'm not mentioning them is I have very little actual recollection of their content and circumstances. I believe that the magnitude of my horror on these occasions activated some sort of emergency self-preservation system which declared martial law on my brain and promptly ordered the neurons retaining the memory of the event to commit suicide. All I'm left with today is the recollection of suddenly realising the full magnitude of what my third finger and the Enter key had just done to me and the extreme desire in that moment for my life to end immediately.

There is, of course, no recovery from a fatal crosspost. In the instant of their occurrence, one is usually completely aware that, following the optional grovelling apology, the crosspostee will never be spoken to again. Their name must be added reluctantly to the growing list of people we're resigned to acknowledge would not only be likely to run us down if they happened to spot us walking alone on a country lane, but would actually be justified in doing so. Any attempt to recover even the smallest fraction of the previously held relationship will only result in the degradation and further humiliation of both poster and postee: any hugs, praise and compliments, any statements of self-flagellation, any intellectual attempts to undermine, counter-argue or in any other way rescind the offending comment made – humorous or otherwise – will ring more hollow and more false than a politician's pre-election promise; never, under any circumstances, should this be attempted. Accept the new reality and move on.

I'm joking, of course. Recovery is indeed possible. You should be warned, however, that the possible grain of truth in your flippant comment, made for the sake of a moment's worth of positive affirmation from the person you thought you were talking to, is likely to become the catalyst for a new level of relationship that involves open articulation of the neuroses you might previously have wished person X had some awareness of, but which you'll conclude were probably better left unexamined after all. By means of compensation, you'll then feel the need to share some of your own insecurities in return; before you know it, you'll be listing each other in your profiles as SL siblings, bound together by the pain of existence in a cruel and unfair universe, and threatening the ten courts of hell on anyone who "messes" with the other.   In the long term, then, it might ultimately be far less pain and hassle to just let the crosspostee get on with the business of thinking you a complete and utter turd from this point on in both your lives.

Returning to the issue of 'fatal crosspost' the phrase as opposed to fatal crosspost the experience, the invention of any new piece of terminology is only really meaningful if other people go on to use it. The difficulty with this particular phrase is that it contains within it – through use of the word 'fatal' – a strong acknowledgement of the magnitude of the deed's consequences that only a person who's committed it can really fully appreciate. To anyone who has not thus far committed this crime (enjoy your smug innocence whilst it lasts), 'fatal' must seem a bit disproportionate, a bit of an over-exaggeration, a bit – dare I say it – 'drama'. They might consider the phrase 'accidental crosspost' to be entirely sufficient a term, not in need of any embellishment or sub-categorisation. A person who chooses to use 'fatal crosspost', then, is sort of admitting through so doing their own guilt. It's a bit like announcing to all who are present that you're the sort of person who routinely talks about others behind their back.

The good news is that, by the same logic, this will only be apparent to other offenders, who will likely nod their heads solemnly in RL and welcome you into the brethren of convicted FC felons. Just as some of you reading this will be wondering what on earth all the fuss is about (whilst others will be smiling at the resonance and simultaneously shuddering at the brief re-emergence of heavily repressed memories), the innocent bystanders will scratch their heads in puzzlement, shrug the phrase off and take their next step on the journey towards their own fatal crosspost appointment – because we're all of us human and we all occasionally gossip. Then, and only then will the true meaning of the phrase reveal itself to them.

If you belong to the group of people who've committed fatal crosspost, can I ask you to do this veteran SL resident a favour and start using it in your conversation? The thing to remember is we're not *really* bad people for having done this, particularly if the words we use to describe it convey that we know that it was wrong and we do indeed feel shame.

30

Immersion matters

First published August 2013, AVENUE Magazine

Much ado is currently being made about the Oculus Rift, a virtual reality headset currently under development and being fitted out for Second Life. Or rather, SL is currently being fitted out for it, with a Rift-enabled version of the viewer scheduled for public release in late summer. There have been significant steps forward in SL visuals in recent months, what with the switchover to server-side avatar rendering promising to assign blurry avatars to history, and the recent introduction of 'New Materials' (my ballpark reading of which is 'advanced bump-mapping') enabling more realistic surface textures. Factor in the buzz surrounding the Rift and there's this faint feeling of stars lining up for a possible second age of SL. I'm not entirely sure how SL will work inside the Rift (I don't know, for example, how typing will be done), though it's easy to see the attraction of this new layer to SL's secret ingredient: immersion.

Immersion is already the thing that, for the vast majority of us, makes SL work. Somehow or another, when we see our avatar in a house or on a beach or in a club or in a shop, there's a part of our mind which treats these digital constructions as though they're actual three dimensional spaces which we really are occupying. Our awareness of our real life surroundings becomes reduced and our attention becomes focused on the objects and people surrounding our virtual representative.

What's perhaps most astonishing about metaverse immersion, however, is that it *doesn't* appear to require especially sophisticated visuals. Although we might always imagine a more graphically beautiful SL to be a better experience than that which we are currently enjoying, when I look back on my own sense of immersion in SL it's not at all the case that it has increased only as a result of improvements to the graphical environment. Some of my fondest memories in SL, in fact, are of locations constructed from prims and textures which, by today's SL standards, really wouldn't drop any jaws in aesthetic appreciation. The town centre performance area in Cookie, for example, is a build so basic it consists to this day of just a simple stage and a collection of single prim seats, yet it's still one of the most real places that exists in my SL.

A couple of weeks or so after joining SL, I was exploring the sims surrounding my birthplace region of Bear and came across an art gallery. What surprised me about this visit was the feeling later on that day that I'd actually visited an art gallery rather than just viewed a representation of one (as we might by looking at pictures in a book or seeing a gallery on the television). Thinking back on it now, I realise a number of important things happened during that visit. Firstly, since my camming skills were still pretty basic back then, I examined paintings on display just by walking up to them. In other words, the behaviour of my avatar mimicked actual 'art gallery behaviour'. Secondly, I had my very first SL conversation there with another visitor, at least a few lines of which were about the exhibits. In other words, I had a conversation with someone that was appropriate to the context of the setting.

It occurs to me now that this occurrence encapsulated some of the vital component parts of immersion in SL. First of all, *places with a specific function increase immersion*. The graphical complexity of these places isn't as important as the function itself, though it would be disingenuous to suggest it adds no meaningful embellishment whatsoever. Second, *functional places where other people act in a contextually appropriate manner increase immersion*. If other people in an SL gallery or an SL café or an SL poetry venue behave in the broadly defined manner that one might expect others to behave in such places, they start to become more real. To put it another way, people 'buying in' to the function of a place makes it work.

For example, kitchens. People creating in SL virtual homes that are essentially the RL house of their dreams is one of the things I found perplexing in my first few months in the metaverse. What on Earth, I asked myself, was the point in creating a kitchen or a bathroom in SL? What was the point in having virtual cupboards that could store no objects and virtual shelving that could hold no books? Initially, I ascribed this behaviour to an absence of imagination. Later, it occurred to me that, in building houses, residents were essentially creating a set on which they could enact their social interaction. In building a kitchen, then, they were providing themselves with a space where spontaneous, informal conversation might take place. It had function. Knowing that a certain space was intended to be a kitchen influenced the sort of behaviours that happened there.

In the creation of familiar places, what we seem to be doing is building areas that allow us to import into SL our RL patterns of social interaction. Of course, this is a far from perfect thing –

especially if we interact with friends from different cultures, where such things as kitchens might have subtly different associations – but it's enough of a hook to make talking with someone in a kitchen or a bedroom or a library feel qualitatively different from talking to them in an open field or – for that matter – talking to them in a Facebook chat box. Places in SL provide an unspoken context to our interactions.

The third component part of immersion to be found in my art gallery example concerns the movement of our own avatars, a dimension so subtle it includes all the things we're not doing as much as it does the things that we are. In real life, for example, I find dancing at parties a vastly undignified act which I avoid at all costs. To see Huck 'getting down' at a club or event is to see a stranger that I don't associate myself with. To see him standing at the periphery, however – the awkward attendee whom everyone suspects is secretly counting the minutes until it's socially acceptable to leave – is to see myself. It resonates.

Immersion isn't, of course, only about finding SL comfort zones that echo RL habits; it's also about exploring new ways of being. I might not like the idea of dancing at clubs, but what better place to become a little more comfortable with the idea than in SL, where I don't have to worry about my rubbish dancing skills, the possibility of knocking into someone, my perspiration levels and the question of if my jacket has been stolen? Whether or not this can ultimately impact on my ability to dance in RL is another question – perhaps that gap is still too large to bridge with current technology – but perhaps the most important issue is less the transference of SL behaviours into RL and more the way that we think about them. I might previously have rationalised my non-dancing behaviour with a belief such as 'All people who dance are idiots'; it will be a bit harder for me to hold on to such a view if I become a regular groover at SL parties.

That said, the current research interest into mirror neurons – recently identified cells in the brain which activate on seeing human movements performed as though we have performed them ourselves – might have a great deal to teach us in the near future about how SL and RL movement interrelate. An article this year in New World Notes told the story of Fran, a senior citizen suffering from Parkinson's disease who has experienced an improvement in her movement since she started using SL. "As I watched [my avatar doing Tai Chi]," Fran reported, "I could actually feel the movements within my body as if I were actually doing tai chi in my physical life [...] For a year I have sat and slept in a motorized lounge chair that brings me to a standing position when I push a button. [...] Now, I can go from a sitting to standing position without even using my arms to push against the arm rests." Claims like this should always be treated with caution until research has had a chance to explore them systematically – indeed, the researchers looking at Fran's case are keen to highlight her own remarkable qualities as a person in terms of the role they might have played in this improvement; as an indication of how much there is yet to learn about the potential impact of immersion in virtual worlds, however, the story has enormous merit. The Oculus Rift, incidentally, doesn't necessarily denote a step forward for people like Fran if it imposes a first person perspective (in the manner of 'mouselook' on current viewers): if you can't see clearly your own body movement, mirror neurons will presumably have less to tune in to.

I still walk up to exhibits in art galleries, even though I could easily cam everything from one spot. That said, if I visited a gallery and there was no-one else there, I might well be tempted to cam. When others are present, I am pushed towards context-appropriate behaviour. A fourth component of immersion, therefore, might be the knowledge that others can see and judge us, activating our responses to being in the company of others (whatever they might be). Human beings are ultimately social creatures: it is to the ways that technology facilitates and frames our interactions that we should look when discussing immersion, not just the visual appeal.

31

The withheld smiley

First published September 2013, AVENUE Magazine

The written word, as we all know, is a wonderful thing. As it has done over the centuries, it constantly shapes and remoulds itself to suit our contemporary needs. What fascinates me most of all about text communication is the ingenious ways in which we bend it so that it includes the very non-verbal information it's supposed to lack.

Perhaps the most obvious and well-known way of doing this shorthand today is through the use of smileys. Those cute little sideways faces are an easy way of showing happiness, amusement, cheekiness and sarcasm, although technically they're not as such an employment of the written word (they've elbowed their way in). Of course, smileys exist for negative emotions also; but the thing with negative smileys is they're not quite really, well, negative enough. The very word, 'smiley', after all, hardly sits with any attempt to express genuine anger or despair; whether it's a sad-faced open bracket you're using or a thin-lipped lower-case l, negative smileys are still just too cute and clever to be taken all that seriously. Using them to communicate genuine states of displeasure is a bit like announcing you've been made redundant through an arrangement of alphabet noodles. For all their valiant efforts, they're ultimately best suited to expressing the milder side of negativity, such as inconvenience or a smattering of frustration. "That book I ordered by Huckleberry Hax still hasn't arrived yet :(". That sort of thing.

When it comes to real annoyance, real anger, real miserableness, we turn to a different, far more subtle set of strategies. Whenever we're feeling *really* low, after all, we lack the energy and emotional literacy to simply tell people what we're feeling – and don't pretend you don't know what I mean. Instead of simply saying how we feel, we offer up clues to our dearest and closest so that they might infer our emotional state. In RL, these clues are relatively obvious and include: The Silent Treatment, stomping about, applying significantly more pounds per square inch than required when returning objects to a surface. And so on. In text, it's a lot harder. Smileys are still a notable part of our strategy, but they're now notable chiefly through their absence: when we're *really* pissed off in text, we withhold them. All of them. Deciphering the meaning of an absent smiley is a complex issue. Here is my brief guide to this art form.

The Greeting Without Smiley (GWS)

Withholding smileys can be a very powerful form of expression, particularly in the initial IM greeting. There are two essential forms of this action. The first – opening an IM exchange without a smiley – is relatively moderate in its severity as a face slap. Starting a conversation, then, with:

Someoneyouknow Resident: hi

is usually a communication that translates along the lines of, "I'm feeling low and I'd appreciate it if you ask me how I am (I'll probably reply with, 'I'm fine', but rest assured any negativity you then subsequently experience from me will be far less than if you hadn't asked)." Receiving such a message when you weren't expecting it is often accompanied by a feeling no more serious than "It looks like a significant percentage of my carefree evening in the metaverse can be written off, then; I suppose I'd better ask what's wrong."

The Reply Without Smiley (RWS)

The second form of this strategy, however, is far more biting. This is to wait for your close friend or partner to greet you with their own smiley and then to reply without one:

> You: hey there :)
> Someoneyouknow Resident: hey

Depending on the closeness of the relationship you have with your correspondent, this could mean anything from, "I denounce your generally cheerful state as naïve, bourgeois ignorance of the pain I suffer; I doubt very much you could have the merest hint of insight into it" to "You, buddy, are in serious trouble". The length of the pause between the greeting and the reply is especially significant: too long, and the recipient might assume the sender to have been AFK or in another conversation, their non-smileyness connected to an entirely external issue; too short and the apparent eagerness to deliver the absent smiley might be inferred by the recipient to mean that the sender was strategically waiting for the greeting, their non-smiley reply prepared and awaiting the fall of the enter key – it might just possibly be a bluff, a pretence at anger to distract from a deeper issue:

> You: hey there :) [thinks, "If I start cheerful, she might feel less threatened by a conversation about why we've not been spending time together recently"].
> Someoneyouknow Resdient: hey [thinks, "If I fake anger over him being on half an hour later than usual, perhaps he won't ask me difficult questions"].

The Reply Without Smiley is the wrong-footing technique of the text conversation world; it leaves the smiling initiator suddenly knowing they've completely misjudged the direction from which the correspondent is coming and defenceless to make any sort of powerful return. To the Greeting Without Smiley, of course, there is always the option to reply in kind, to answer the sender's grimace with your own: "I'll see your pain and match it," you can nonverbally reply; the opening moves of a game I refer to as 'Pissed Off Poker" (POP):

> Someoneyouknow Resident: hi
> You: hey

But to the RWS, any attempt to imply your own annoyance following that initial smile – that gawping, inane, frankly idiotic grin – is certain to be met with failure. A smiley smiley, once offered, cannot be taken back.

Adding extra bite to the withheld smiley

Veterans of POP will know that there are, of course, a number of additional techniques to strengthen a RWS or own opening gambit. Capital letters and full-stops (or 'periods', as I understand they're called in the US) are one such play. Restraint from the use of familiar forms of greeting is another.

> You: Hello.

is, therefore, a hard GWS that signifies trouble and only trouble lies ahead for the recipient. On the other hand:

> Someoneyouknow Resident: hi
> You: Hello.

is the POP equivalent of "I'll see your pain and raise you my misery". Finally:

> Someoneyouknow Resident: hey there :)
> You: Hello.

is the ultimate in RWS replies – less of a slap across the face and more of a punch to the nose – and to be used very sparingly. Incidentally, those of you who insist on initial letter capitalisation and full punctuation in every IM you write might like to rethink this approach: your 'Hello.' will be greatly diminished in its power as a result.

[Even more incidentally, whilst we're on the subject of literary pedantry, if you're one of those people who just can't lower yourself to the pictorial arrangement of alphanumeric characters, "/me smiles" is *not* the grammatically correct equivalent of ":)" – the fact you've gone to the effort of typing the extra four characters makes it a non-spontaneous smile; thought through; calculated; possibly insincere. Don't like that? Go to the extra effort of writing "/me smiles warmly" or "/me smiles in delight" then.]

Responding to the withheld smiley

What options remain to the recipient of a RWS? It all depends. There will be those times when your reaction to one of these is a genuine 'huh?' and a frantic searching of recent memories for clues of something you should feel guilty about: profiles will be hurriedly examined for their rez dates (if you can enter a "Happy Rez Day!!" within ten seconds of a RWS, you might just pull it off as an unresearched comment; you can be fairly certain, however, that you'll be in a busy region in such moments and profiles will take no fewer than 90 minutes to rez), IM logs will be rapidly scrutinised for mention of RL issues you should have attended to better. If nothing is discovered, one option is to take the 'standby gambit' and just await a further response (depending on the circumstances, this will either reward you with an eventual comment that strengthens your position – since it betrays your partner's desire to speak with you – or it will result in a silence until logoff for which you will pay dearly at a later date – probably with your life). Another is to overcommit to happy smileys in every subsequent comment as some sort of stubborn, post-hoc rationalisation of cheerfulness, slapping them merrily to the end of every sentence visible. For example:

You: hey there :)
Someoneyouknow Resident: Hello.
You: how are you? :)

effectively says, "I refuse to succumb to your attempts at reducing my well-earned positivity". It's a bit like those Facebook picture-quotes on happiness and love and not changing that you sometimes find yourself wishing you could roll into a cone and use to stab the poster in the eye.

But there will also be those times when you know full well why you haven't received, won't go on to receive and – quite possibly – don't deserve to receive a smiley in reply to your greeting. To this, I can only ask, why the hell did you open with a smiley in the first place? Talk about just asking to be slapped.

32

Some more novel ideas

First published November 2013, AVENUE Magazine

November is with us again, the month in which hundreds of thousands of people each year turn their backs to orange-coloured October and sink all their free mental capacity into the writing of a fifty thousand word story. I'm talking about National Novel Writing Month, of course: a cocoon-like period of time out of which one emerges bleary-eyed and startled to find that Christmas has somehow arrived. I started in 2006 and I've only missed the finish line once since then. Actually, last year I was ten thousand words short by 30 November, but I did at least go on to finish that title and 'AFK, Again' – my fifth novel set in Second Life – hit my virtual bookstore in March of this year. That's a plug, by the way. You can buy it.

Last year in this column I had a lot of fun dreaming up potential SL storylines for novels. Unashamedly, I intend to do the same again here. I've long believed, after all, that the potential for metaverse fiction is vast (my meagre offerings are but a scratch across the surface). Here are just a few humble suggestions.

Occulus Thrift. As the global financial crisis deepens, more and more people turn to the metaverse – now reborn through virtual reality headsets distributed through a government depression reduction initiative – to escape the poverty-stricken decay of their real lives. Bit by bit, society transfers itself into this second world: physical schools are deemed too costly to maintain and teachers face obligatory transfer to virtual equivalents; public transport is closed down in line with new policy that actually seeing in real life your friends and relatives is now a luxury activity. Finally, even, parliament itself is shut down as an unnecessary expenditure, elected officials moving into a dedicated sim custom-built to include a 1000 square metre debating chamber and a 5000 square metre lobbyist parlour. Into all of this enter Aramatter Fisk, a young student of domestic history (specialist subject: Tupperware) who accidentally discovers a whole extra hidden world being developed by the wealthy elite. Thinking at first that he's stumbled across a 1950s cold war experiment (a hypothesis that fits absolutely none of the available facts, but which appeals to him as a fan of the pre-1958 Tupperware sale to Rexall), Fisk attempts to open peace negotiations with the first residents he encounters. The Overlords – as they call themselves – take him immediately into custody and charge him with treason, but Fisk escapes by taking a plane to a rival faction within the same metaverse. Granted asylum, he then sets about the task of revealing to the world the true nature of its digital government; meanwhile, the Overlords impeach their President on the grounds that he didn't do a good enough job of making the rival faction scared of him. Following a thrilling chase scene, the novel ends on an anti-climax when The People respond to Fisk's news with a nonplussed shrug and comment that they'd pretty much figured something like this was going on anyway.

Far from the Madding Prim. A novel set entirely in a single region called Wessex. Although a walk along the country lane that connects up East Wessex with West Wessex would take in real time about a minute, the narrative is padded out into a seven hundred page volume through the protagonist's description of every prim he observes along the way. Every. Single. Prim.

You've Got IMs. This metaverse RomCom (alternative titles: *Sleepless in Second Life* or *Love Virtually*) telling of the clichéd *boy meets girl, boy loses girl, boy runs into girl by accident a few months later at a hair fair and she can't slip away because of the lag, girl turns out to be boy, boy turns out to be girl, boy(girl) and girl(boy) get married* tale lulls the reader into a false sense of security four fifths of the way into the novel, then plunges him/her back into uncertainty at the shock revelation that both boy(girl) and girl(boy) are in their nineties. Somehow or another, through avoiding too many age-appropriate cultural references and by throwing in the odd mention of iPhones and Miley Cyrus, they have successfully given the impression that both are professionals in their twenties involved in IT startups. They arrange to meet in RL, choosing Brighton Pier as their rendezvous. When Adam(Felicity) realises that the chosen date clashes with his(her) scheduled hip operation, he(she) cancels the medical appointment, only for Mary(Bill) to then get offered a date for her(his) own hip operation because someone else cancelled at the last minute. In RL, Felicity hobbles painfully along the pier and eases herself down onto the empty bench they were supposed to meet at. With just two paragraphs to go, the reader assumes all is lost, but then the agreed pass phrase is whispered from behind her and Felicity closes her eyes and smiles. The book closes on this happy, tear-jerker moment, although the astute reader will note that Felicity is still expecting at this point to open her eyes and see a man seventy years her junior. Possibly, this intellectual cliff-hanger will be debated in internet discussion forums. Possibly, it won't.

Downton Primley. Another attempt at a period SL novel. This time, the story revolves around Baldwin, a servant in the estate of Mr Robert Primley, Earl of Lindham. In addition to managing the estate staff, Baldwin is also the Head Builder for this metaverse role-play affair. Not only must he see that afternoon tea is served on time, he also has to hunt down period appropriate textures every time Lady Primley decides that the china needs replacing. Whilst our hero struggles with his employers' ever-increasing appetite for authentic mesh furnishings, he is witness to an illicit affair between the Earl's visiting brother, Sir Marcus Primley, and nineteen-year-old chambermaid, Agnes. Four months later, Agnes comes down from the servants' quarters wearing a second trimester pregnancy bump which she's resolved to display at luncheon. Sir Marcus is visiting again, en route to his Cornish residence in Penzance, but this time he has with him his wife (who's taking the advice of her physician and leaving London for a short, restorative break of three months). Agnes plans blackmail. Baldwin tries to talk her out of it, knowing what the Earl's brother is capable of, but the naïve young girl goes ahead with her plan anyway and is found hanging from her bedroom rafter the following morning (her account hacked by the evil Sir Marcus, who is in reality the CEO of a large Android software company). The novel ends on this tragic note, Baldwin musing philosophically, whilst he supervises the morning laundry, that Edwardian period role-play represents the top of a new slippery slope in society's moral decline.

Murder in Prims. Franklin Berkowitz, a deeply eccentric yet wildly successful designer of state-of-the-art mesh avatars, decides to give away his entire catalogue – including his next generation, full facial animation range, 'AVXL' – in protest against Linden's new terms and conditions. He announces this plan to his real life and metaversian business partner, Mark

Warburton, over a Martini in a piano bar in downtown LA. Warburton is aghast, for the AVXL range is set to take the virtual world by storm and earn them a ton of cash. When he realises Berkowitz is serious, he arranges to meet the following night to discuss the giveaway strategy (telling Berkowitz not to speak a word of his intention until they've had the chance to plan it properly). The next night, Warburton murders Berkowitz, making it look like a suicide. Enter Lt. Columbus, an Italian-American police detective who smokes cigars and wears a crumpled raincoat (and is legally distinguishable from any similar fictional detectives by a nervous twitch that presents whenever fish are nearby). Feigning incompetence at anything remotely digital, Columbus lulls Warburton into a false sense of security, then irritates the crap out of him by constantly turning up in SL to ask him questions about the metaverse. A typical exchange goes something like this:

Columbus: This is your house, sir?
Warburton: Yes Lieutenant.
Columbus: And you built it?
Warburton: Every last prim.
Columbus: This is really something. This is really something.
Warburton: There was something you wanted to ask me, Lieutenant?
Columbus: Oh, yes, sir. Just a small issue. I have to fill out these reports, you know…
Warburton: Of course.
Columbus: I was just wondering… something I just can't figure out about the gunshot… And this couch? You made this couch too?
Warburton: Yes, Lieutenant, I made the couch.
Columbus: Did I tell you my cousin makes real couches?
Warburton: You didn't. Something about the gunshot, you say?

In the end, it turns out Columbus had Warburton identified as the murderer within three minutes of entering the crime scene from the position of the walnuts on the coffee table. The novel ends with our hero reaching a decision about what sort of gift to buy his wife as an anniversary present, a comedy theme threaded through the plot including one scene where he convinces Warburton to build him in prims a faithful replica of his own mantelpiece so that he can see what various ornaments will look like on it.

33

On faking your death in SL

First published December 2013, AVENUE Magazine

There ought to be a word for when a comment left in response to a Facebook friend's post piques your curiosity enough that you click on the commenter's name to see what other sorts of thing they've written elsewhere (I make no apology for this snooping; I'm endlessly interested in how people express themselves online)... and a resulting chain of profile hopping ensues as you move from comment to profile to comment to profile, a sometimes hour-long exploration of random people you've never met connected only by the thread of your happenstance curiosity. 'Browsing' doesn't quite capture it for me, somehow. 'Browsing' implies you're waiting to find something of interest, whereas this little bounce from personality to personality reveals new fascinations with every single step.

One such carefree hop and skip across Second Life Facebook profiles a few months ago led me to a comment about a man who was described as having died in RL some time ago, only to return in SL about a year later. I've heard about this sort of thing before, but never actually met someone who did it. Also, I was under the impression that people who 'came back' tended to do so in a new account so that they didn't get found out (although, of course, they usually did get found out because they just couldn't resist getting in touch with old friends in their new persona and giving themselves away through their textual mannerisms; it would be nice to think that the number of people who use 'u' instead of 'you' in SL do so only to distract from signature phrase slippage and that it hurts their soul to do this just as much as it does mine to read it). I did a web search on this returned avatar's name and found several posts across various forums about his RL death, plus a couple of later – less than complimentary – confirmations that he was, in fact, alive. I looked up his profile inworld and saw that he is indeed currently active. He made no comment there about his earlier 'death', but there was a mention of sending those who didn't "understand" him to a dark and fiery place.

Why would someone do such a thing? Just to be clear here, I'm not talking about people who tell everyone they're leaving SL and then later return – we all have a right to change our minds: what I'm interested in are cases where a person goes out of their way to give people the impression that they've died in real life. I don't know how this was achieved in this case, but a number of potential methods come to mind. One could log in as an alt, for example, and pretend to be an RL friend of the deceased; one could send emails as a family member according to your 'dying wishes'.

It turns out that faking your own death on the internet is sufficiently significant and old a phenomenon that it's been researched. As an example of 'Munchausen by Internet', a term coined by Dr Marc Feldman (thanks to Mistletoe Ethaniel's very informative blog post on the topic - http://tinyurl.com/qxvw9hl - for pointing me to this), the prevailing hypothesis on faked internet death appears to be that the main motive for doing this is to inflict emotional pain on people, perhaps some sort of revenge for actions they have previously taken or as a gauge by which to assess how much you were loved. I've personally never heard of such a thing actually happening within my own SL, although I've certainly seen emotional blackmail used in spades – including someone hinting about considering killing themselves in RL in response to the actions of SL others. Hinting is a long way from actually doing, of course, but then – well – so is pretend doing.

Dare I say it, but could another rationale be to get out of an unwanted relationship? We can criticise such a strategy for being cowardly, but we've all been in a situation where the noble, the sensible, the intelligent thing to do feels either completely impossible or – frankly – too much bother. Breaking up with someone because they're insecure and needy, for example, is an insanely hard thing to do without a) leaving them feeling criticised and worthless, and/or b) becoming a cold, uncaring bastard. How much more easy must it be to simply die, terminating the relationship and leaving the ex-partner grief-stricken, but with their self-esteem and the memories of their love intact? If you're *really* into the rationalisation of being a total shit, you could even argue that the bereaved might end up this way with a better sense of perspective: it's the win-win approach to breaking someone's heart.

Perhaps the reason for faking one's death in SL that I have the most empathy with, however – and I should probably add at this point that I'm not considering this as an option; if you should hear that Huck's driver has completed his mortal doings, you can be relatively certain that this is genuinely the case (although if I was planning to fake my death I suppose I *would* say that) – is the possibility this offers for witnessing the reaction to your demise. Perhaps 'empathy' is the wrong word; what I mean is that I can understand the curiosity people might have about the esteem in which others actually hold them. After all, how often do we actually tell people whilst they're still alive what they mean to us? However many irritating Facebook memes on floral backgrounds we see telling us to do this, it's just not a thing we're comfortable with; we save our best, our most comprehensive praise for people until after they're gone.

I should point out that I see a clear distinction between this reason and the *Munchausen by Internet* motive outlined earlier: were I to contemplate such I thing (I'm really not, ok?), it wouldn't be to measure my worth by the size of others' pain; it would be out of a genuine curiosity to know what people thought of me. I have no idea what impact I've had on others as Huck. I have a few friends who I'm reasonably certain like me more than they dislike me, but beyond that I really don't have much of a clue. And what about my novels? Would they receive some sort of posthumous recognition denied me denied me during life? I can't deny that makes me curious.

Of course, one of the reasons why we don't hand out praise whilst people are still alive is that no person comes in a package of good qualities only. Whilst someone's still alive, their negative attributes are often just as visible as all the positives. Whilst positive attributes such as notable achievements or generosity continue to be true after death, however, negative issues pretty much cease to be a concern. If I'm considered to be impulsive, temperamental and unpredictable whilst alive, for example, my capacity to shock and upset pretty much stops the instant I pass away. That truth becomes less meaningful posthumously than the truth of my achievements. To put it another way, how we think about people is different after they've died than whilst they're still alive; it's not necessarily the case that people are withholding what they think of you whilst you're still around.

So what I hear people say of me at my virtual memorial might not be what they think of me whilst I'm still alive; that doesn't mean to say, of course, that I'm still not curious as to what it might be. And this is where an RL faked death really comes into its own in SL, for where else on the internet could you find an actual gathering of people collected for the sole purpose of paying tributes to a deceased friend? Comments on a discussion forum is one thing, but an event held in your honour at a place and a time is where SL claims the trophy on online remembrance.

But a note of warning for anyone who mistakes this piece as an instructional article: be careful what you wish for; people don't always celebrate the deceased. You might put on your very best alt and very best suit and very best black tie and turn up to your virtual memorial to find yourself the only person there. You might even discover that no-one was especially moved to hold one. Don't be too surprised to discover that you have no friends if they meant so little to you in that first place that you were prepared to let them think you'd died.

34

The second life of Second Life

First published February 2014, huckleberryhax.blogspot.com

Depending on who you listen to, Second Life is either taking its last few gasps – hence the departure (voluntary or otherwise) of CEO Rod Humble – or is getting ready for new life to be breathed into it via a renewed interest in virtual reality (VR). The commercial release of the Oculus Rift headset is potentially less than a year away and VR is starting to become a hot topic once again in the industry. In the last couple of weeks alone there has been the news that Steam owners Valve are putting their weight behind the Rift and foresee VR becoming a consumer reality by 2015; meanwhile, Yahoo! have bought out and closed down virtual world Cloud Party and lit the fuse on rumours that a Yahoo! metaverse is in the pipeline.

The edge that SL is likely to have when the Rift launches is that it's already compatible with the headset and could presumably be accessed through it just as soon as it's out of the box. If you're lucky enough to be unwrapping a Rift on Christmas morning 2014, therefore, but don't have any compatible games to use it with, you'll be able to plug it into a free SL account right there and then. Indeed, if the Rift does make it to the Christmas 2014 market then 25 December this year could just be the laggiest day in SL history. But don't worry – I'm sure Linden has a plan for that.

Of course it all depends on how big the take-up for the Rift actually is and who the buyers are (let's not forget there are age restrictions for accessing SL). But let's assume for the moment that the rumblings of VR being the Next Big Thing are correct and SL sees a surge of new users keen to try out their new hardware on what, to some extent, could be considered the freebie game included in the box (the VR equivalent, if you like, of 'Wii Sports' only without your grandmother playing bowling). Whilst most of us would welcome new interest in SL (for two reasons: 1) a bigger user base might stimulate greater investment in SL, both from Linden and from third parties, and 2) more people using SL might mean that the rest of us don't need to feel quite so socially outcast in admitting our residency and trying to make it sound better by using such phrases as, "I belong to an online community"), would this actually constitute the holy grail of mainstream involvement that's so far eluded our aging virtual world?

It's been argued that SL's long-term problem has been less about attracting new users and more about keeping them. The resulting focus on user retention led to a new viewer design intended to be easier for the newbie to use (and which you'd be forgiven for thinking was the coming of the anti-Christ from the reaction it got from long-term residents), some noncommittal talk about making the grid accessible via a web browser and a number of attempts at making the first half hour as straightforward and as interesting as possible. None of this addressed the issue of lag, which became the big, grey, unrezzed elephant stuck in the corner of the room that we were encouraged not to talk about since there was very little that could be done about it in the era of ADSL connections. For me, however, this was always the biggest barrier. The one RL friend I managed to coax into SL lasted no more than forty-five minutes because he could only see puffs of floating smoke for avatars and couldn't move an inch from the spot he landed in; the interface he had no problem with at all.

But the ADSL era is now starting to come to an end. Whilst SL on a fibre-optic connection doesn't cure lag *completely*, it's undeniably a better experience. During the very long wait for this we've had all manner of graphical improvements added, and the metaverse now looks a great deal more beautiful than it did back in the day when SL was last a topic in mainstream discussion. But will all these improvements be enough to retain the hypothetical virtual reality newcomers?

If the Rift does take off, there will be plenty of other companies keen to grab for themselves a slice of this virtual, cash-filled pie. The games market, of course, will be a big part of this and whilst initial titles – if history is anything to go by – will probably be Rift-enabled versions of existing games, any momentum built from this could stimulate big players into hunting down the 'killer-app' of VR. We already know of Philip Rosedale's 'High Fidelity' project, and the Yahoo! Acquisition of Cloud Party just *might* be the beginnings of an exploration of social media in a metaverse. But these things are potentially pebbles: if VR really does become the Next Big Thing then it will be less a question of who is developing for this new media than who isn't.

What, then, will keep Rift-enabled newbies in SL if the IT world starts throwing its weight seriously upon new VR projects? There have been many graphical improvements made to our world – yes – but a lot of these have that screwed-on feel of medium density fibreboard and require a lot of work – not to mention an advanced SL skillset – to achieve. I'm aware of such things as mesh heads and mesh hands and mesh feet as the new must-haves for fashion-conscious avatars, for example, but which newbie is *seriously* going to spend time on lining all these things up precisely and getting the colour matching right? Which newbie is even going to know about stuff like that? Whilst SL is *capable* of more stunning avatars than it used to be, then, Rift-enabled newcomers are likely to look decidedly more blotchy and lumpy, and probably even more so when viewed up close and in three dimensions through a virtual reality headset. Yuck.

Iris Ophelia wrote recently on New World Notes (http://nwn.blogs.com/nwn/2014/01/world-of-warcraft-avatar-revamp.html) about how World of Warcraft has updated its avatars, and very succinctly summarised the problem that Linden would have in doing a similar thing: whilst higher definition avies in SL would undoubtedly look much better, they'd break a huge percentage of existing SL wardrobe and cause outrage amongst residents. Perhaps, then, the only way forward is through all-mesh avatars, and from the moment that the new user signs up. But, rather than making SL a more attractive place for recently arrived residents, such strategies are really only considering how to reduce its ugliness; more a thinking about fixing the things that might turn people off SL rather than creating the things that might turn them on to it.

Alongside trying to figure why it is that many people leave the metaverse quickly, then, it might just be worth spending a little time considering why it is that some don't. Speaking personally, whilst SL was just 'an online game' to me I felt no sense of attachment to it whatsoever; it was only when it started feeling like a collection of actual places that the addiction began to set in, and the time leading up to that point I spent achieving very little and wondering what on Earth the point was in it all. For those of us who stick with it, our ultimate sense of immersion in SL comes not from the graphics environment as much as it does the sense of connection to the places and people we find. Second *Life* is entirely the wrong name for this package: it's a second *world* we discover, in which our one and only life gets itself a little bit more space to exist in than we previously thought possible. When it does capture us, it's because SL has taken us by surprise.

The things that build this sense of connection to virtual places include the events that take place in them. I've visited countless art galleries in my time in SL and open mic venues and bars and clubs and theatres and learning spaces and role play regions; what's made them most real are the exhibition openings and readings and concerts and performances and award ceremonies (yes, really) and meetings and classes that have happened in them. The more I think about it, however, the more I become convinced that the single biggest thing that keeps me most rooted in the metaverse is having a home there. If only SL were like Facebook or Twitter or Blogger or any of the other social networking phenomena where it's been worked out that giving folk a free little bit of it to decorate and call their own is one of the key ingredients to making it sticky. What's needed in SL, I think, is a free basic home for all users.

I know this will likely never happen, but it won't not happen for technical reasons when a physical place in the metaverse is only storage space and processor time on a server somewhere; it will likely not happen because of the politics of it all, and the outrage and the vitriol which will probably make going peacefully into liquidation appear a much more attractive and dignified option. Which is a shame, because the free home wouldn't have to be big: with today's low impact mesh, it should be perfectly possible to furnish a basic skybox for what we old timers would call 50 prims and people who wanted more than that could buy or rent the extra space the old fashioned way.

For years now, wannabe commentators like me have been making such pie-in-the-sky claims with the freedom to make them as unrealistic as we please. Like the UK Liberal Democrat Party, you can visualise all you want when you're not ever going to be in a position to have to make any of it actually happen. Where things are different now, however, is that we're approaching a possible threshold point where that dreamed of mainstream metaverse might actually be lurking round the corner; if there is serious money to be made from virtual reality, people *will* be looking for the model which resonates most with what people want. Competitors bringing new products to the market really won't give a damn about doing in their world the things that in SL would incur the wrath of land owners or content sellers or any other resident who thinks maintaining the status quo of their business model is more important than preventing their whole world from going bankrupt.

If SL can't adapt then the likelihood is it will be overtaken. The coming of the Oculus Rift, then, might well usher in Second Life's greatest ever moment in the light; it might also, however, herald the beginning of its end.

35

Metaverse and Death

First published March 2014, huckleberryhax.blogspot.com

In my upcoming novel, *Beside an Open Window*, human beings make regular digital scans of their brains while alive so that these can be activated in a vast online world once they die. The book is set sixty years into the future and 'dead residents' interact in this world with living residents who access it in much the same way as we do Second Life today.

The idea of creating brain scans is one I've been thinking about for several years. Sometime before SL existed, I remember wondering if it might one day be possible to create 'archived' copies of brains on computers. It was less an issue to me at the time that we might do so in order to extend in some way human existence and much more that we might do this to prevent the loss of people's thoughts and memories. I think this had a lot to do with the death of my father, who I missed profoundly and whose thinking and experiences I considered a genuine loss to his fields of interest.

When I got into SL, the idea that such archives might connect to the metaverse – and thereby have natural movement in a virtual world – was very compelling to me. I hadn't put a great deal of thought previously into how digital brains might interact with the world, oscillating broadly between a very basic 'brain-in-a-jar' scenario where an archive was switched on periodically for electronic consultation and the full-blown (and, frankly, unlikely) 'holodeck' notion promoted in Star Trek. Somewhere in the middle of all that I'd also thought fleetingly about uploading brain scans to robots – an idea I later discovered was explored by Janet Asimov in her novel, 'Mind Transfer'.

In a virtual world, however, a brain could roam about with freedom in a virtual body and consume only a fraction of the energy and costs of any robot or far-fetched holodeck idea.

Could such a thing, then, actually be possible? There are a few conditions which would have to be met. Firstly, it would have to be possible to scan a brain at a resolution able to identify individual molecules. Memory is stored via pathways through different neurons, the route that an individual signal takes through them being determined by the quantities of neurotransmitter chemicals passing across the tiny gap between one neuron and the next – the synapse – and the receptiveness of the receiving neurons to these chemicals. Only by knowing the exact state of all of this could we create a scan that was in any way functional. No such technology exists today, although the resolution of brain scanning is continually improving. By interesting coincidence, one recent innovation allowing users to scan and view their brain activity in real-time – 'Glass Brain' – has been co-developed by none other than SL's own Philip Rosedale.

Secondly, we would need gigantic computer memory capacity for storing brain scans. One estimate I read recently was that there are something approaching 500 trillion trillion atoms in a human brain. Assuming this is true and assuming we assigned one byte of computer memory to the description of each atom, my back-of-an-envelope calculations indicate we would need something in the region of 50 trillion terabytes to store all this. Applying Moore's Law to computer memory growth – starting at 8 gigabytes for a mid-price desktop system today – we might predict that the computers of 2064 will have memories in the region of 250,000 terabytes, which is rather a long way short of what we'd need. Add another sixty years of Moore's Law progression, however, and you're pretty much there.

Thirdly, we'd need to be able to bring these scans to life: their data would have to mean something to the computers they're loaded into, just like a jpeg means something and an MP3 means something else. We'd need to understand the precise function of neurons and brain chemistry in order for this to happen, such that each neuron's data description can be turned into a fully emulated brain cell once the model's switched on and digital blood applied. We'd need to know how visual input is encoded in the eye and sent down the optic nerve if we want our dead people to see in the metaverse and how auditory input is encoded in the cochlea if we want them to hear. Sensory input, in fact, would be a huge area for further research: contrary to popular belief, the brain receives input far more complex than just 'the five senses'. For example, shut your eyes and hold your hand at arm's length, then move it towards your nose but stop just short of touching it: how did you know where your hand was in terms of what sight, sound, smell, taste or touch were telling you?

Even supposing we work out how to do all these things, however, there could still be another enormous barrier to emulating the mind: consciousness, without which a human brain is nothing. In *Beside an Open Window* the theory of consciousness as emergent behaviour is assumed. Emergent behaviours are apparently organised behaviours that emerge from the more simple behaviours of large collections of smaller organisms. The seemingly simultaneous movements of flocks of birds or shoals of fish – movements which give the impression of an organised whole rather than lots of disorganised individual components – are examples of this. In science fiction, the idea of higher order behaviours arising out of the more mundane work of component individuals is something that's most famously been explored in Star Trek through the notion of the 'hive mind' of The Borg. Human consciousness as an emergent behaviour of neurons – ultimately, then, an illusion of sorts – is something that 'just happens'… but would it happen also in a digitally modelled brain? That's the sort of thing we can't possibly know until we actually try it out.

Supposing, then, that consciousness does happen, what would existence be like for these resurrected brains? What would they do? What would it be like to live in a digital world and only be able to look back into the real one, as though through a window?

In my novel, the metaverse of sixty years from now is envisaged as a wholly photorealistic environment that looks indistinguishable from the real world. Given the pace of computer graphics development over the last few years, this part of the proposition seems very uncontroversial; indeed, the gold-rush on virtual reality technology that appears to be in play right now – with Facebook the latest large company to jump on this particular bandwagon in its acquisition of the Oculus Rift – would suggest that visual immersion is considered the new holy grail of online interaction.

All well and good if you're a flesh-and-blood human only looking in on a virtual world, but if that world is the only thing that exists for you then you're going to need more than just visual stimulation in order to feel anything approaching complete. As I mentioned earlier, our brains receive input from the external and internal world far more complex than the notion of 'five senses' would suggest. We might consider the notion of 'touch' to be straightforward, for example, but is not the experience of sensing temperature through our skin qualitatively different from the sensation of sensing a surface to see if it is rough or smooth? Also, how would you describe sensations such as a full stomach or a headache in such terms?

In *Beside an Open Window*, digital humans (I read a fascinating article recently by George Dvorsky, in which he discusses futurist Robin Hanson's thinking on the subject; Hanson refers to digital humans as brain emulations, or 'ems') can see and hear, they can feel surface texture and pressure, and they have the sense of proprioception that enables them to move about in a co-ordinated fashion (that's the sense that enabled you to detect when your finger was almost at your nose). They have no sense of taste or smell, however – eating and drinking is not possible – and are unable to sense temperature. They also have no internal senses so they can no longer feel any sort of internal discomfort such as indigestion or muscle fatigue, nor internal pleasure such as feeling (mildly) drunk or the sensation of orgasm.

This might seem like a small price to pay for an indefinitely extended existence, but it's important to consider just how fundamental these sensations are to the experience of being human. Such activities as eating, drinking and having sex might ultimately only occupy a small portion of our total existence time, but our internal sensations are constantly with us and form a huge part of our mental state on a moment-by-moment basis. What would anxiety feel like, for example, without a rapidly beating heart or a knot in the stomach? What would relaxation feel like without that sense of your body being in a state of comfortable balance? How would you know what mood you were in without these associated physiological sensations learned over a lifetime of real-life existence? Would you even experience different moods any more? The approach I take in *Beside an Open Window* is to assume that the brain projects a 'phantom body' in the same way that amputees experience phantom limbs, that specific neural outputs to the body have become so conditioned to the associated neural inputs that the outputs now trigger the inputs even though there is no longer a body attached to them (in other words, the mental component of anxiety is so commonly associated with the physiological component that the one triggers the neural inputs of the other). This is pure speculation on my part and might not be even remotely true. Life in the total absence of internal sensation might ultimately be completely intolerable.

But the brain is uniquely flexible in its ability to adapt to new environments and might just surprise us. Assuming we are able to adapt in this way, then, what might we do in the metaverse once we're there posthumously and, in particular, how would we make money? Whilst life in the metaverse might be cheaper than in the real world, with no food and utility costs to cover, that's not to say there won't be any costs at all. You'll still have a carbon footprint that will need to be paid for and the price of virtual land might get pushed up if everyone wants the mansion of their dreams to live in. You might also have dependents back in the real world to look after.

Whatever metaversian job opportunities exist, there will also be plenty of jobs that deceased, digital humans (DDHs) could be capable of back in the real world. There's no reason why secretaries and personal assistants couldn't be DDHs; programmers could be DDHs, lawyers and accountants could be DDHs, IT support could be DDHs (no great change there). Elements of teaching and medicine could be carried out by DDHs. Sales and customer service departments for large corporations – the future equivalent of today's call centres – could be staffed in their entirety by DDHs. Only the jobs that require people to go outside and manipulate physical things – tradespeople, nurses, front line police, etc – would be safe from DDH competition, though their managers might not be. And you thought automation and immigration were the biggest threat to your jobs.

DDHs won't only be attractive to real life employers because they'll cost less, they'll also be attractive because they'll be faster. There's no reason why an emulated brain couldn't be sped up significantly for all or part of its existence. Programmers, for example, could be run at many times their normal speed so that more work can be done in less time – an attractive option for the programmers themselves if they can switch in and out of speeded up time without noticing anything different themselves (an arrangement could be made, for example, where workers turn up on the hour, do what feels to them like a full day's work and then finish an hour later in real time with more or less a whole twenty-four hours off before their next shift starts). Or you could take a bunch of world-class scientists, speed them up a thousand times and then give them fifty years in a sealed-up metaverse to solve humanity's problems.

The question is likely to arise, naturally, on what sort of rights DDHs have. Would they be recognised as living in their own right? Would they get the vote in real world elections (would they have their own representatives in government)? Would the intentional deletion of a brain scan be regarded in the same manner as murder? Could two DDHs get married? Could a DDH get married to a living human being? If a person is married to someone in real life before they die, is it the assumption that they remain married once activated as a DDH? What if the brain scan was created before the couple met?

If someone dies because of an accident they caused and in which other people also died, would some sort of sentencing need to be carried out against the DDH on its activation, even though its scan was created before the incident (potentially, years before)? What would a metaverse prison look like? If a murderer was sentenced to life imprisonment in real life, could there also be a digital life component to their sentence so that a thousand years really does mean a thousand years?

There might be the temptation to activate your brain scan in the metaverse *before* you die in real life and put it to work whilst you enjoy the qualities of the physical world – they won't, after all, be there for you forever. Would this make DDHs slaves? Would there be legislation against such activity? More generally, how would people get along with the digital replicas of themselves? Which of the two of you would be regarded as the most authentic 'you'? Would you both be partnered to the same person if the copy was made and activated whilst you were in a relationship?

What if you someone activated two copies of their brain in the metaverse instead of one? Or three copies. Or a hundred. What if someone made an illegal copy of a scan and put it to use in some way?

As you can see, the issues are endless; there are many more beyond this mere handful and I am fascinated by them all... which is why I wrote *Beside an Open Window*. To see which of them I explore and to what end you will, of course, have to read the novel. Next weekend, however, as a precursor to the release of *Beside an Open Window* later in April, I'll be publishing here a complete chapter from the book that works as a stand-alone short story and which considers digital life from the perspective of a recently deceased husband and father, and also ponders what it would be like to attend your own funeral.

36

Inventory: Your own personal ticking time bomb

First published June 2014, huckleberryhax.blogspot.com

There are a couple of completely unrelated activities I've become involved in lately that have got me thinking about the stuff we hold on to. The first of these, in chronological order, is the clearing out of my mother's attic. It's a long overdue job and I'm approaching it slowly and methodically, going through everything one box at a time and sorting according to whether each item should be thrown out, scanned/photographed and thrown out, kept, or ebayed. After four, hour-long sessions, I'm approaching the end of my first box and there must be at least fifty boxes up there (most of them much larger than the one I've nearly finished). Many of the boxes haven't been touched in over twenty years.

When I committed to this project, I did so with a somewhat heavy heart and only because I knew that it *had* to be done sooner or later. Much to my surprise, however, I'm actually quite enjoying the task. I've discovered all kinds of things that have brought back memories of moments lost or simply a recollection of the world as it once was through my then more innocent eyes. Letters, photographs, Christmas cards, magazines, things my father wrote when he was alive, toys long forgotten; and so on. It's nice to occasionally reconnect with how things once were, even if only for a few minutes.

The second activity is far less wholesome for the soul. I'm somewhat ashamed to say I've become addicted to the online game 'Simpsons Tapped Out'. Those of you familiar with this app for phones and tablets will know it involves creating your very own version of Springfield by saving up virtual dollars accrued through sending the various residents available on jobs; these dollars can then be used to buy land or construct buildings. All well and good, but the game involves a lot of waiting around because these jobs can take anything up to twenty-four hours for residents to complete, as can building construction. To get around this, you can speed everything up using the second currency of donuts. But here's the catch: donuts can only be bought using real money, and this is where EA Games, the makers of Tapped Out, make their return on the app. Buying donuts is a temptation I've so far avoided, however there are clearly plenty of users who take this approach, since the game – free in all other respects – is reportedly a huge financial hit.

How is this relevant to my musings on stuff? I went to a discussion forum a few days ago to find out what people were saying about a new set of quests that have recently been added to this game, with a whole new set of items than can be earned. People were discussing these with some excitement, and one of them eagerly posted, "I've got them all already with some donuts I got bought for my birthday".

It's a funny old world. I can listen to some truly dreadful news items with the most dispassionate of responses, but for some reason this really hit me. Actually, anything concerning childhood innocence usually does it. I once saw a really aggressive kid I knew taking a glimpse through a crack he'd found in the papered-over window over of a Santa's grotto and the look of childhood joy on his face made me want to blub uncontrollably. I assumed, you see, that this post had been written by a child (I might be wrong) and it upset me that for his or her birthday they had received something they would never one day be able to come across in their attic and hold and feel and smell. One day, Simpsons Tapped Out will be an obsolete title and all these purchased items will be gone. The game doesn't work without a connection to the game server, and when it reaches the point, to quote Troy McClure, where it's no longer profitable, that server will get its plug pulled and everything anyone ever 'owned' on it will vanish.

As it is also with Second Life. Everything in our inventory – everything we think somehow belongs to us – actually resides on Linden servers which one day will get turned off. Everything: every picture, every notecard, every outfit, every building, every piece of furniture you ever bought or made, every trinket and curio, every garden feature, every single hairstyle you've ever worn; one day, it will all of it be gone. You do not own any of it.

Whatever you think Second Life is, it cannot last forever. Whatever improvements are made to it, it will not in the long term be able to compete with new virtual worlds that aren't built on an eleven year old architecture (happy birthday, by the way, SL). Eventually, there just won't be enough people buying land or paying tier or purchasing stuff on the marketplace for Linden (or whoever ends up owning SL, if Linden one day decides to sell it) to make money out of it. Some people will definitively leave; others will drift over to new products and find their visits to the first ever virtual world less and less frequent. Whatever. Whether it's a year from now or five or ten or twenty, that moment must inevitably come. There are things we can export, such as pictures and notecards and any objects we've built ourselves, but more or less anything we've bought or received from others is stuck forever in our inventory, and the stuff we can take out the majority of us will probably never get around to moving because there's just too much of it. By the time we realise we want to keep hold of it because of the memories these things unlock, it will all be too late.

The more and more I think about it, the more I feel a pull towards the conclusion that this inevitable, unavoidable truth is the real reason – or part of it, at least – why Linden changed its terms and conditions regarding ownership of inventory last year. Because we tend only to think in the here and now, this got misread as some sort of nefarious plot to make money out of our intellectual property. I don't think it's that at all; Linden denied this and we've yet to see any evidence to the contrary. But now that most commentators seem to agree that our metaverse is now entering its final age, anxiety at the labs over what rights people have to items in their inventories must have started to grow considerably. Solution: let everyone know that Linden owns the lot so that if (when) they chose to extinguish it, then they have every right to do so.

What, if anything, can be done about this? Experimentally, I've exported a couple of items I made in the past to InWorldz and it worked okay – textures had to be uploaded separately, but that's doable. InWorldz, however, isn't all that different from SL as I understand it, insofar as it's still one central organisation holding all the server space. OpenSim would appear to be a much better long-term storage option, since (as I understand it) you can use it to run your own region on your own PC, rather than having to connect to regions online. Still, this is only a solution for things you have actually made yourself, which in my case would be less than one per cent of my total inventory. And even some of those are un-exportable:

much of my own furniture, for example, uses all-permission sculpted elements I've bought such as mattresses and cushions; using these in my items is entirely 'legal', but, when it comes to exporting, just one of them in an item I've made will block the whole thing from being saved to my hard disk.

Perhaps, between now and the end of SL, someone will come up with some sort of magic tool – a deus ex machine to my prophecy of doom – that will allow the export and conversion of everything to some new virtual world we're all emigrating to. I'm not technically knowledgeable enough to know whether such a thing might be possible, but even if it is it's likely to cause an outcry among sellers, who have been fighting the copybots for years. It would probably get banned.

We should probably reconcile ourselves, then, to saving what we can while we can. For my part, that will mean saving my snapshots to hard disk and maybe trying to take a few more pictures than I ordinarily do in the time we have remaining. Regarding objects, the vast majority of my stuff is junk I no longer use and I suppose it won't be the end of the world if it should all pass into non-existence. Like so much stuff we get rid of in real life, pictures of it will suffice. There are a few gems here and there, however, which I will really, really miss: the first home I built (it included cheap bits and pieces I picked up from dollar stores), my unbelievably cool 70s bed (not actually finished as a saleable item yet, but you simply have to see the furry leopard skin cover), the neck chain my best friend Dizi made for me from a maze design (carved into stone at a place in Tintagel) when I told her how much I liked it.

I would love one day, years from now, to come across these things in a virtual box in a virtual attic so that I can look at them for a while and enjoy the memories they evoke.

But I'm pretty sure that I won't.

37

Linden Lab announce a successor to Second Life

First published June 2014, huckleberryhax.blogspot.com

The breaking news yesterday on Wagner James Au's always excellent New World Notes was that Linden Lab were first rumoured and then confirmed to be working on a successor virtual world to Second Life. In a statement sent to the site, Linden said that the new, 'next generation' world will be "an open world where users have incredible power to create anything they can imagine and content creators are king. [It] will go far beyond what is possible with Second Life, and we don't want to constrain our development by setting backward compatibility with Second Life as an absolute requirement from the start" - meaning it likely will not be compatible with SL and any inventory you have will not transfer over. They do go on to add, however, that this "doesn't mean you necessarily won't be able to bring parts of your Second Life over, just that our priority in building the next generation platform is to create an incredible experience and enable stunningly high-quality creativity, rather than ensuring that everything could work seamlessly with everything created over Second Life's 11 year history."

Big surprise? Not really. I speculated earlier in the year about the coming age of virtual reality – which, let's all take a deep breath and remind ourselves, could yet turn out to be as actually popular as 3D TV – and how this might give SL a boost in popularity because it's essentially a free product out of the Oculus Rift box; part of my speculation was that whatever the take-up is, however, it will probably only be short-lived: Whilst

SL's various bolt-on upgrades over the years have undoubtedly improved its graphical appeal hugely, these are finicky things that require skill and experience to organise, and many newbie VR explorers, therefore, just won't get the experience we know is possible. Something better – and a great deal simpler – is needed, and SL will only endure as a popular VR virtual world experience so long as that alternative doesn't exist. If Linden don't supply this then someone else will.

Other than reporting that the new world is only in its "very early" stages and that the company is "actively hiring", Linden doesn't give much information about the status of this project. Potentially, it's entirely conceptual right now (although it's tempting to wonder if there is any flow of information between Linden and *High Fidelity* via Philip Rosedale). Whilst this likely means that the new world is potentially years away at this stage, getting the word out to SL's core user base that something new is on the horizon might just help keep them loyal whilst other tempting products start to appear. It's ultimately a much wider user-base than this that Linden will want to attract, but long-term SL residents will include the skin-makers and the clothes designers and the furniture builders and the landscapers without whom any serious attempt at a user-content driven world will fail.

What I find most interesting about the statement are two things. First, the use of the phrase 'next generation' suggests a new reframing of business at Linden. Former CEO Rod Humble previously reframed the company's work as making 'creative spaces', an ethos which resulted in a veritable tumble of products into the marketplace which were thought to fit this brief – dio, Versu and Blocksworld to name but a few. Any of those that failed to turn a profit got swept away quickly and brutally when current CEO Ebbe Altberg took up the reigns (although Versu got a new lease of life recently following an outcry from fans of Emily Short when it emerged that her Magnus Opus for the interactive fiction platform, *Blood and Laurels*, was complete and unreleased) and with this new announcement we're seeing Altberg stamp his mark firmly on what many of us have been feeling of late is a somewhat ailing franchise. 'Next generation' is a phrase we're used to seeing in connection with such markets as mobile phones and games consoles and mobile data networks, business areas we also associate with a large range of products. The use of this phrase, therefore, signifies not just a step forward in technology but also Linden's acknowledgement that we're now moving into an era where they will face something they have never previously encountered: serious competition. Over the eleven years of its existence, there have of course been a few alternatives to SL crop up here and there, but none have attracted anything like SL's numbers. This time, however, it's different, and Linden's experience in this field will not necessarily give it any more advantage in the approaching market than Nokia's experience did when Apple popularised the Smartphone. The question has to be, are Linden acting fast enough, or will they become yet another market leader that failed to respond in time to the developments in its own field?

Second, I find the phrase 'content creators are king' especially meaningful, and it gives me hope that Linden have actually tuned in to what has made SL, in its own words, "the most successful user-created virtual world ever." In a fractured metaverse of competing virtual worlds, content will become the new apps of this market. As we have seen, time and time again – VHS versus Betamax, Blu-ray versus HDDVD, Windows Phone versus Android and iOS, to name but the headliners – content is what wins format battles. I can think of no better combination for developing rapidly an attractive content base than straight-forward tools and an open system for user-generated content, and the means to make money out of it. User-generated content has made SL what it is and any new virtual world product which fails to take into account this tremendous success – and which fails to put it at the very heart of its philosophy – is unlikely to make any long-term impact. When you stop to think about it, user-generated content is what gave *MySpace* the edge over social networking pioneers such as *Friends Reunited* (anyone remember them?) and then *Facebook* over *MySpace*.

But what excites me most of all about this announcement is the sense of new energy it communicates. Has Altberg managed to shake Linden out of its fatigue and re-inject some of the pioneering spirit we all miss from the old days? I sincerely hope so. Now needs to be a time of group huddles and fist-bumps and air punches and battle cries at Linden HQ. If it all comes to pass as the pundits are predicting and VR really does become the Next Big Thing in the IT world (again – deep breaths – it might not), we will be faced with a whole range of competing worlds and experiences; the very notion that Linden *wouldn't* be there with its sleeves rolled up and slugging it out confidently with the newcomers is alarming. Second Life is an amazing product and its architects *should* be diving in to whatever is approaching: they have earned their place there.

I'll reiterate now my (previously expressed) belief that the company has to rethink its policy on land if it's going to achieve a mass-market appeal in its future ventures: content is great, but you need somewhere to display it and nothing roots you to a world more than having a home there. Hopefully, these early days of the construction of 'Second Life 2' will include a period of reflection on what's been learned from SL that will include such issues.

There is, after all, so much that has been learned. SL always was a product ahead of its time, but that time is now approaching. In years to come, we might look back on our current world as ultimately the testbed pilot that led to a metaverse as pervasive as Facebook, as inspiring as nature, as unifying as sport and music. Get in there, Linden: no-one knows this business better than you do; make us the place we have all been dreaming of.

38

Could an office in Second Life 2 be the killer app that virtual reality is looking for?

First published July 2014, huckleberryhax.blogspot.com

Now that everyone's panicking about the atomic bomb dropped by Linden last month when they announced their successor to Second Life (which, I'm now given to understand, has nothing whatsoever to do with competing in a suddenly rapidly expanding market and is just the next step in the company's mission to screw residents in every last way achievable), I thought it might be a good moment to start thinking about the ways in which a 'next generation' virtual world could differ from the present one.

A new metaverse which works in broadly the same way as the present one – albeit with better graphics, less lag, and full immersion via the Oculus Rift – might sound like a good thing, but would it really capture the imagination of the masses? A lot of us thought that 3D cinema was a new and amazing thing when Avatar was released a few years back, but when it came to buying a 3D TV, few people could really be bothered and Nintendo's 3DS handheld games console – complete with its built-in 3D camera that would enable us all to record our moments in stereoscopy – completely failed to capture the public's imagination (though, admittedly, not as much as the Wii U did). If SL2 really is going to capture the attention of hundreds of millions of people rather than just millions of people, as Linden CEO Ebbe Altberg has recently claimed as its objective, it will need to bring with it something genuinely new.

The same is true of VR more generally. In my mind, one such thing is objects with function.

Many objects in SL do already have function, but it's an extremely limited function. You can sit on a chair. You can lie on a lounger. You can open a door. You can close your blinds. Perhaps the most sophisticated functional object I've seen so far is one of those fancy television screens that links to channels showing old movies or which can play YouTube videos: it's a method for watching something with someone, for sure, but it's hardly bringing into being something that can't be done outworld. No. The sort of function I'm thinking of is far more complex.

Just over a year ago, I was fortunate enough to get a short tour of future concepts being developed by IBM. These included a facial recognition system for use in commercial environments (remember those billboards in Minority Report that changed when Tom Cruise walked past them to show him personalised adverts? - that technology exists right now) and a remote control toy car that you can drive with your mind. But centre stage for me was the big black table in the room with a surface that acted like a giant iPad. If it had actually just been a giant iPad it wouldn't really have impressed me all that much; what blew my mind was the way in which it was possible to manipulate documents on this thing: you could spread them all around you like pieces of paper, you could tap one to bring up a localised keyboard alongside it for editing; when you were done with it you just pushed it to one side for filing. We've seen similar fictional systems to this in movies like Quantum of Solace and, more recently, The Amazing Spider-man 2; what I saw at IBM was nowhere near as whizz-bang as either of these, but it was real and – by God – it worked.

I'm particularly excited by technology such as this because for years I've struggled with the concept of the 'paperless office'. I've been interested in computers for over thirty years now, but my enjoyment and knowledge of them hasn't stretched so far to any acceptance on my part for replacing paper in my everyday work. Sure, I use a PC to write reports and emails like everyone else, but the moment two documents are required for any particular job, I start reaching for the print button. To give you an example, when I'm marking an essay I need to see both the essay itself and the marking grid I use: I could switch between them on my PC screen, but I dislike doing so intensely. I want to see them side by side, so I end up printing both essay and grid, completing the latter by hand and then later typing it up. It's an inefficient way of working, I know, but it's the best fit there is for the way in which I need to think. For people like me, then, the interactive surface I saw at IBM represents a way in which the paperless office could actually happen.

But do I see such technology turning up in regular office spaces such as mine in the near future? I do not. The cost is likely to be prohibitive without a mass market to sell to and a mass market is likely going to be very difficult to establish when – quite apart from anything else – people are living in smaller and smaller spaces. If 3D TVs costing hundreds of pounds were a difficult sell, I hardly imagine interactive tables costing thousands or tens of thousands of pounds are going to walk their way into people's dining rooms.

But virtual reality might just be the way through which people like me could access this way of working, and at a fraction of the price. I sit at my regular table or desk and put on my Oculus Rift and activate/teleport to my office in the virtual world: there I'm sitting at an interactive desk where I can spread all my electronic documents around me and work on them in the manner that suits me. So what I *feel* through my fingers is the surface of my real life desk, but what I *see* is my interactive desk with all its documents and applications. The system would of course be linked to a cloud storage account so that I can access outside of the metaverse the work I do inside it: swiping a document into a particular folder on my desk would store it in – let's say – my Dropbox account, so I would then be able to bring it up in the real world on a PC or tablet.

There would be other benefits to working this way. Rather

than being an isolated room, my office in virtual reality could be connected to the virtual offices of all my co-workers so that we could use the interactive desks for meetings or joint working. Whole buildings could be constructed in the metaverse for individual companies or organisations: buildings where people actually work rather than the business-themed dolls' houses we see in SL composed of empty room after empty room. Working from home would never have to be the solitary thing that it is now, where contact with other people comes in the form of emails and the occasional phone call.

Is current technology up to this? I don't know. I've not had any experience so far of using a virtual reality headset, so it might be that my expectations don't quite match the reality of this technology as it stands at the moment. It might be, for example, that the graphics resolution isn't quite so good that I'd be able to read the text on documents comfortably without enlarging it significantly or bending over to see it. Also, in addition to the headset, some sort of device would be required for reading my hand and finger movements. I know that the Microsoft Kinect is capable of reading body movement, but I don't know whether it's fine-tuned enough to do so sufficiently well to distinguish between different virtual key presses or to be able to keep up with my typing speed. A system that constantly produced typing errors because it was only 99 per cent accurate would be infuriating.

Then there's the creation of the document management software itself. Whilst not beyond the scope of technology today (as I saw at IBM), this would be no small issue: it would effectively be the creation of a whole new operating system, the sort of thing it takes Microsoft, Apple and Google years to develop (and, in the case of Windows, still get wrong). I say it wouldn't be beyond the scope of technology today, but there I'm thinking of a system for use in real life: implementing such a thing in a virtual world would require an inworld scripting system light years ahead of what's achievable with something like Linden Scripting Language. And it would require lots and lots of processing power.

But this is future-gazing, and from the vantage-point of a period in time that's not even yet the beginning of the virtual reality era. Whatever does start to emerge next year, it will be certain to be improved upon quickly. And it's been acknowledged by the current architects of virtual reality that VR as yet has no 'killer application' concept that might make it a must-have rather than a novelty or niche interest. The first ever killer app, incidentally, was VisiCalc, the first spreadsheet program (for the Apple II computer). Can you imagine working life now without spreadsheets or any other the other killer apps that succeeded them, such as word processing software or email?

I realise you were probably hoping for something a little more exciting from the metaverse than yet another reworking of the way you use a word processor, but it might just be that one day you can't imagine working life as possible without your virtual reality office.

39

The continuation of division

First published September 2014, huckleberryhax.blogspot.com

Those of us old enough, wise enough or, essentially, unhinged enough to have seen between the cracks of this big brick wall we call 'society' will likely long ago have worked out that there's no such thing as the new product that will make everything better; nor will there ever be. The next new iPhone, we've realised, will not cure the world of ill and it won't do a single thing for an individual that even the most ardent of Apple fanbois would select to look back upon fondly in his very last moment of life. Likewise the next Xbox and the next PlayStation and whatever it is that Nintendo does next. Likewise, in all probability, the Oculus Rift. Likewise Second Life 2.

All of these next-big-thing bandwagons, we've realised, are essentially just the dressed-up treadmill of capitalism, the soap opera gift-wrap to the requirement that we endlessly buy things in order to keep everything (and everyone) working. This is no big revelation anymore. Even the machinery of capitalism itself no longer tries to conceal it from us; there is no need. It turns out that most of us are no more turned off from buying things when the inner guts of consumerism are exposed than we are from eating bacon when we learn it comes from pigs.

How we love looking forward to our next big tech, just the same. The rumours. The anticipation. The debates. The reviews. That we know (in the same way that know the Earth orbits the sun and not the other way round) that this is all just an endless loop and that this time next year it'll be something else we're looking forward to diminishes our enjoyment of it not one jot. I'm not being cynical here: I enjoy it all as much as the next moderately IT-informed human being. And I'm not saying either that no things created are transformational, just that they're not really transformational *enough*.

The computer, for example, has been transformational; I still marvel at word processing. The Internet has been transformational and I still marvel at email and the speed with which I can pull information from the web on just about any topic in a matter of seconds. Perhaps the most transformational thing of all about the Internet, however, is the communication it opens up with other people. It was *inconceivable* when I was growing up in the seventies and eighties that we would in the not-to-distant future be able to speak with people all over the world for as long as we wanted and for free – let alone video chat with them. Even throughout most of the nineties this seemed unlikely. Today, it is more-or-less taken for granted.

Second Life, in its admittedly rather clunky fashion – although I have no doubt this will be improved upon in its next incarnation – takes this one step further: In SL, we can actually *do things* alongside people who are hundreds or even thousands of miles away from us. We can create together. We can perform together. We can watch things together. We can shop together. We can just sit together if we want to in a café or a living room or a town square or an open field and talk. It is *astonishing* the boundaries that the metaverse enables us to transcend.

In theory.

If I could travel back in time to make a visit to my teenaged self and describe to him the world's technology today, I wonder what he would say? Let's suppose I arrived in early November 1983 when, unbeknownst to most of us at the time, the world came within a button's press of World War III. Nuclear annihilation was something I thought about a great deal in those days and it sobers me to think that there are in all likelihood a great many parallel universes in which Soviet nerve did not hold out and the world really did end that week. On 7 November 1983, *Uptown Girl* by Billy Joel was at number one in the UK music charts (incidentally, the first seven inch single I ever bought) and *Islands in the stream* by Kenny Rogers and Dolly Parton topped the US Billboard Hot 100. In the news, a bomb was exploded by a terrorist group at the United States Senate (no-one was killed). It was a Monday. I would likely have spent the evening playing on my *ZX Spectrum* computer. Can you remember what you were doing that day?

In truth, right then I was only just becoming aware of the nuclear threat and the likelihood is I was far more preoccupied with what was happening in *Doctor Who* than I was with world affairs (after all, the twentieth anniversary special, *The Five Doctors*, was just a couple of weeks away). If the button had been pushed, I would likely not have understood what was going on (not that I would have had all that much time to digest it), which is probably how it should be for a twelve year old boy. Even so, if a forty-something me from the future had turned up to talk about the internet and things like Second Life, I like to think that I would have worked out pretty quickly that a consequence of all that incredible communication potential *had to be* that people were finally managing to get along together. Well, wouldn't it?

But, in 2014, despite all these transformational advances well beyond the scope of what most of us who were around 30 years ago could have dreamed of, we're still about as far away from that dream, it seems, as perhaps we've ever been. As nationalism sweeps across Europe (the rise of the *UK Independence Party* in the UK is only one example of this), as Russia takes what many feel to be the first of many calculated steps to come in rebuilding the former Soviet Union, as the US is slowly torn in two by increasing political polarisation, as *Islamic State* – arguably the love-child of the Blair-Bush legacy – bring unspeakable brutality to the middle east, I'm waiting for the moment when people on big stages start asking the question, *Why? How has it come to this? How have we not yet moved on from here? Why have we not made some sort of progress when we have all this incredible technology?*

It's too easy to blame just the politicians. As an inclusive humanist, I have long been waiting for the world leader who has the courage to explicitly make decisions based on the world's interests rather than "this country's interests" (whatever that country might be), but I'm not so naïve as to believe that such a person wouldn't be voted out of power at the very next chance his or her electorate got. It's too easy to blame the people of the press, who sicken me on a weekly basis with their seeming quest to make us angrier and angrier and angrier; it is us, at the end of the day, who buy their newspapers and sustain this. It's too easy to blame parents. It's too easy to blame schools. It's too easy to blame capitalism. It is all of these things together – and more – and the whole is so much greater than the sum of its parts.

And yet, it's really not so complicated. All we have to do – all of us – is be better at empathising with others and exercising compassion. That's it. That's all we have to do. Pretty much every single disagreement I've ever been witness to has involved one or both sides being unable to understand how the other is thinking and feeling.

In recent months, I've become excited in my anticipation of yet another potentially transformational moment to be brought about by technology. Over the last couple of decades, our knowledge of planets beyond the solar system has exploded: as of 1 September 2014, we know of over *1,800* worlds, with new ones being discovered at an astonishing rate. We have the *Keplar* telescope to thank for much of this, a $500m NASA spacecraft that enables astronomers to identify planets when they move between us and their native star. Like so many NASA missions, its operational life has already far exceeded its planned life expectancy and the data being returned has enabled estimates on the number of potentially life-supporting worlds in our galaxy (calculated from the percentage of solar systems which have planets of a certain size orbiting their sun at a distance which would expose them to a comparable amount of solar radiation to Earth – it turns out this is about 20%); currently, this number is thought to be *in the billions.* This analysis has become increasingly refined and new techniques are being devised which will allow analysis of the atmospheres of these planets. One such technique will enable astronomers to detect the presence of chemicals known not to exist naturally in the universe. When the day comes that a world with these chemicals in its atmosphere is identified, we will have discovered proof of intelligent life on another planet. There is a growing confidence amongst scientists that we will have this proof within the next twenty years.

Perhaps this discovery will be the catalyst that changes human thinking from 'me' to 'us'. For many years – perhaps decades; perhaps centuries – we won't know anything about these civilisations other than that they exist. We won't be able to communicate with them (the distance will be far too great); we won't know what the people of these planets look like or what they eat or how their homes are or what their art is like: we will only know that they are there. We will only know that we are not all that there is any more. We will only know that all of us on this planet are one thing – human – and that there are now other beings we know of who are not this thing. We might finally start to identify with the people we previously hated.

And yet it's so terribly lazy to pin all one's hopes to a magic solution from a far-away place; as a writer, I can't help but feel I'm just hoping for a *deus ex machina* to pop out of thin air and rescue us all, and that I should be shamed for the very thought by having my pencils taken away. And even if it happens, it might in any case turn out to be no more transformational a moment in the long term than was the release of the Nintendo Wii; humans are incredibly wedded to their prejudices.

But something has to happen if we're going to survive. We can't just continue with our them-and-us mindsets indefinitely and expect things to all work out somehow. Every single time we call someone a jerk or take sides or add to the polarisation of a debate; every time we make it harder for people to rethink their positions and meet us (or others) in the middle ground, every time we collude with the idea that one side is right and the other is wrong, we only end up digging ourselves deeper and deeper and deeper. It isn't easy, but neither is it complicated. I don't really know how Second Life could help us build some of these bridges, but I still believe that it has the potential. It's not going to be a menu option, however, or a HUD you can buy on the Marketplace. All SL can do is provide the opportunity.

Whilst I've been writing this article, the former Northern Ireland First Minister Ian Paisley has passed away. Dr Paisley was a big man who, for many years, placed himself in an entrenched position over the future of Northern Ireland. His later decision to fight for peace and share power with his former bitter enemies was a turning point for the Northern Ireland peace process and the key moment for which he is being celebrated now in the media.

Peace is never without pain, and Northern Ireland remains a stark example of this. But peace is peace, and we have to fight for it. If we don't, the eventual alternative will be so much worse than whatever wounds we have right now.

40

Is sex in Second Life pornography?

First published October 2014, huckleberryhax.blogspot.com

Wagner James Au has opened up an interesting debate over on his blog, New World Notes, stating that Linden should "forbid pornography and extremely violent content [on Second Life 2], at least in the first few years of launch before SL 2 achieves mass growth (assuming it does)." This is based on the finding that half of SL's current most-visited regions are adult-themed.

All credit to Au for having the courage to even approach this can of worms, let alone open it. On the one hand – as was swiftly pointed out in the comments that followed – this statistic could be interpreted in a very different way: that the popularity of adult sims suggests SL2 absolutely *must not* ban such content if it wants to achieve appeal. On the other, however, many long-term residents – myself included – are sick of the sniggers that mention of SL gets amongst RL friends; sniggers based upon the widespread belief amongst the 'masses' that sexual activity is the main reason why people enter the metaverse. Of course, we all know that plenty of people do enter the metaverse for exactly this reason, and also that plenty of people who don't go on to discover it anyway. I have no real issue with that at all, but I do wish SL could be respected for all the other experiences it offers – or at least that it could be understood as a place where people get up to the same range of stuff more or less that they might in any other place. As Au goes on to say, "virtual porn in particular has always been an impediment to Second Life going mainstream, hurting its brand, scaring away mainstream institutions, and just generally causing it to be a laughingstock for anyone who wasn't familiar with how much more non-porn content the world contained".

What really got me thinking about Au's piece was the notion that sexual activity in the metaverse could be termed pornography. To be fair, whether it can or cannot is something of a straw man issue not really relevant to the larger point he's trying to make – possibly for want of a better word, he's using the term 'porn' as a convenient umbrella for activity he's absolutely right in highlighting has given SL an unhelpful reputation.

As a side issue, however, I think it's still one worth exploring. Porn is an ugly word. Folklore would have us believe that something like 99 per cent of men use it, yet if that is the case it's certainly not as openly discussed amongst this population as its other passions, such as football: the knowledge that it's widely used does little to reduce the sense of personal shame or embarrassment in admitting to using it oneself. There's plenty of evidence to suggest that regular ejaculation in males promotes good health in a variety of ways, so one might think that anything which facilitates this could be viewed – at least tentatively – as a good thing (not everyone is lucky enough to have a sexual partner, nor necessarily one with whom sex is frequent enough to achieve these benefits). But the word porn carries with it an immense baggage of association, with mental infidelity, the exploitation of women and the maintenance of male chauvinist and misogynistic views probably headlining amongst these.

An argument could be advanced that 'porn' is no longer fit for purpose as a word which carries sufficient meaning by itself. One qualifying adjective has already fallen into common use, with 'child porn' now the common expression for a *type* of pornography which is illegal. There's a clear and necessary need for this (much as we would wish that there wasn't), a line which just has to be drawn. Other lines or subdivisions aren't perhaps as necessary, yet to classify, for example, a video of two lovers having consensual sex (which they've both agreed to distribute) as the same thing as one of an acted out encounter between a plumber and a housewife (who has mislaid her purse somehow) seems odd; we wouldn't consider a home video of a family barbecue to be the same thing as a restaurant scene in a movie just because both featured people eating. To extend that category into some of the more extreme areas of pornographic depiction and practice makes the one-size-fits-all approach feel even more bizarre. And what about porn made by women? What about porn made *for* women? What about 'revenge porn' videos posted after a break-up? What about the videos made with the explicit purpose from the start of publically humiliating someone? What about beautifulagony.com, where no nudity or sexual contact whatsoever is shown, only the faces of people as they experience orgasm? Is all of this really one thing? Surely not.

Though this, to a certain extent, is also another issue. What about sex in Second Life?

Perhaps sex in SL can be considered under two different lenses. First of all, there is *the depiction* of sexual activity: the poses, the animations, the removal of clothing, the visual enhancement of genitalia through attachments, the use of furniture or other items, the sound effects and the various descriptive phrases used either by the people engaged in the act or – and I still scratch my head over how this phenomena came into being – by scripts in the aforementioned genitalia; all of the things which someone could observe, either as a person involved or as a third party witness to the scene. What sets this aspect aside from 'conventional' or 'traditional' (I really can't think of a better summarising term) pornography is that it's an entirely artificial depiction: anyone observing such a scene is not actually observing real people actually having sex. Having said that this is different from 'regular' porn, however, computer generated sexual imagery is certainly not an invention of SL and goes all the way back to the very earliest and least graphically capable of computers, where 'pixel sex' would have referred to black and white pixels the size of your thumb. Beyond that, erotic drawings and paintings pre-date computers by centuries. In this respect, then, perhaps SL sex can be considered pornographic.

The second lens, however, concerns *the interactive nature* of sexual activity in SL. If one is engaged in sex with another person in the metaverse, one is no longer a passive observer of an act. Instead, one is actively engaged with another person in creating sexual imagery – be it through a visual depiction as described above or through an entirely textual exchange of intimate thoughts and ideas. Whilst there might be elements of this which originated in SL, the more general notion of interacting with someone non-physically to create a 'sexual story' is, again, hardly unique to the metaverse. 'Sexting' – the act of interacting with someone sexually over mobile phone texts – is perhaps the most prominent example of this discussed in the mainstream media today (whenever a celebrity or politician gets caught doing it), but, going back, sexual activity took place in internet chat rooms long before even Yahoo Messenger became popular – before even the web was created. Then there's phone sex. Then there's sexually explicit letter-writing.

Whilst publically expressed opinion on such activity might well be judgemental, such judgements would probably mostly take place in the context of a revelation of someone who is in a monogamous relationship interacting sexually behind the back of their partner. A politician caught doing this is only generally newsworthy if he or she is a married politician. Amongst the liberal-minded, at least, few would raise much of an eyebrow upon learning that someone was sexting their girlfriend or boyfriend – it might well be considered a little Too Much Information, but no more so than learning something about their 'regular' sex life. Few would consider it *porn*.

Does role-play blur the issue still further? In a role-played situation, a fictional scenario is created between two or more people; the option to share RL information alongside this is of course there, however it's entirely possible – and, I understand, an expressed preference amongst some role-players – that a whole scene could be acted out without any reference whatsoever to the authors' emotional state or sexual arousal. In such a scenario, the argument could be forwarded that the only sexual intercourse that takes place is between the avatars on screen as fictional characters, that the real-life humans behind them are merely writers engaged in an act of shared storytelling. Is this still, nonetheless, the creation of pornography? Even if all authors involved remain completely sexually detached from their narrative, they are still creating something which depicts a sexual act, as described earlier – even if it's entirely without avatar manipulation (an entire scene could be role-played in chat or IM, whilst avatars remained fully clothed, potentially not even in the same sim as each other).

By this reasoning, then – and I readily admit it's a tentative reasoning; others might approach this from entirely different standpoints – sex in SL both is and is not pornography. One of the reasons why I continue to love Second Life and the metaverse more generally is the way in which it opens up topics like this and exposes the inadequacies of the words and constructs we use to define life and the experiences which comprise it. 'Porn' is an inadequate word. One of the most beautiful things about sex in SL is how it can awaken you to the thoughts, feelings and desires of your partner – and that's something you can take back with you into the real world if you hadn't already discovered it there.

To return to Au's article, if SL do implement a ban on porn in SL2 it will be a hard ban to enforce. Animations and poses would all need to be vetted, for starters (including all scripted furniture). Nakedness would need to be forbidden, perhaps by incorporating underwear into all skins, though this would require all user-generated skins to be vetted also – in fact, more or less anything worn or attached would need to be checked in order to avoid the creation of 'nudity clothes' (which I recall reading once was the method of circumventing enforced-underwear employed during the days of the teen grid). For the ultimate in porn-prohibition, chat and IM would also have to be monitored, perhaps using the same sort of software that corporations now use to screen emails (your IM to someone that you can't sleep because the cock next door is crowing would be blocked with an automatic message that "Your message breaches our community communication policy"). It would be an enormous effort that many might argue would be better invested elsewhere.

And yet, sex in SL is an issue. In fact, it's not whether or not it's 'porn' that's the issue, but the sort of sex that's going on and where it's happening. By and large, I think the division of sims we have today into adult, moderate and general – with adult sims separate from the mainland – is appropriate. Remember: at the time of SL's largest media exposure, sex halls could be wondered into within your first few virtual steps.

But the issue is ultimately deeper than that. There are sims and groups in SL which promote rape fantasy. There are sims and groups which promote female slavery and humiliation. I've heard the liberal arguments about consensuality defending these things, but I remain deeply uncomfortable about their existence in the metaverse.

My guess is that a ban on sex – or porn, if you prefer – in SL2 is probably unlikely. If virtual reality does go on to become the Next Big Thing, however, expect the can of worms concerning it to get well and truly opened.

41

Yet more novel ideas

First published October 2014, huckleberryhax.blogspot.com

November is nearly upon us, that month when the world's population of fictional characters is incremented by at least a million as aspiring writers across the globe sharpen their pencils and set to work on dragging the novel inside them kicking and screaming onto the empty page. If you don't take part each year in National Novel Writing Month – or NaNoWriMo, as we veterans like to call it – then you don't know what you're missing. What else, after all, is there to do in this muddy, overcast month; this dour, humourless security officer of a month who beckons you in from the warm oranges of October only to keep you waiting in cold, windy dampness for what seems like an eternity before finally unhooking the rope which admits entrance to the delights of December? In the UK, we try to liven up this bleak collection of days with bonfire night, supposedly once a celebration of a terrorist's failure to blow up the Houses of Parliament, but possibly actually just an excuse to remember what being warm felt like. In the US, the artificial bubble of enforced gratitude generated for Thanksgiving collapses so spectacularly on the day after that news coverage of the blood lust of Black Friday has now become important entertainment viewing the rest of the world over. Anything to make the month pass more quickly.

But November novel-writers are oblivious to all of this. Enshrined in their little cocoons of their very own make-believe, the only possible relevance of happenings in the real world to them are if these can offer any potential plot devices. Time passes all too quickly when you're trying to knock out 50,000 words in a mere thirty days, though this is not to suggest that there won't be moments when you wish no-one had ever invented the concept of the novel or writing or language even itself, and that an impromptu world war would at least have the silver lining that it might spare you from having to think about any of these things ever again.

For the past couple of years in AVENUE magazine I've entertained myself (and, possibly, one or two readers) in November with a collection of potential storylines for Second Life inspired novels, that emerging genre of fiction across the surface of which I've vainly scratched away for the past eight years. For my own amusement as much as anyone else's, therefore, I humbly present yet another.

Lindependence Day. The continent of Nautilus decides it wants independence from the rest of Second Life and manages to convince Linden to hold a referendum of its citzens. The campaign is ferocious. All attempts by the board of governors to persuade Nautileans to vote 'no' only seem to increase the percentage saying to the pollsters they'll vote 'yes' – even Ebbe Altberg's surprisingly emotional plea not to vote yes just because it represents a possibility to "kick the effing Lindens" has Yes campaign leader Nigelex Salmage claiming that the No campaign is falling apart. In the end, even Philip Rosedale is wheeled out to make the case for 'Better Together'. Salmage is unperturbed; speaking with absolutely no authority whatsoever, he claims that an independent Nautilus would keep the Linden as its currency and that residents will still be able to access Torley Linden videos. In the end, the reality of independence is brought home to the majority when several high-profile mesh creators start talking about relocating their skin factories to Zindra.

Project Really Interesting. Comedy. A bunch of high-school nerds create the perfect female avatar and she comes to life in the real world thanks to a keyboard spillage during a thunder storm of something cutting edge (let's say a memristor-graphene suspension) that one of the gang swiped during a school trip to the local science genius's laboratories. It turns out that the very same genius has been secretly plotting to take over the world and our heroes manage to put a stop to his plans through a sequence of contrived events that mostly require one or all of them to be naked accidentally. A zany caper from start to finish; if this were a movie you could expect it to be advertised on buses during a holiday season.

The Amazing Second Life into Darkness. In a not-too-distant future, the successor to SL is launched by Linden. Marketed as a reboot rather than a sequel, 'Amazing Second Life' features planets rather than continents and sims, with travel between worlds a lengthy, complicated and expensive affair. Whilst your initial rez point is officially described as random, it soon becomes clear that Linden are employing a formula which the company eventually fesses up to being derived from your Google search habits, your Amazon spending pattern and the number of times you've shared pictures of Grumpy Cat on Facebook. Group identity being what it is, however, the revelation comes too late to prevent entrenched identities from forming and, within barely a year of the new metaverse's release, two nearby planets go to war over a mesh body IP issue. It is the first in a decade-long series of conflicts which historians later refer to as The First Virtual War. Property is destroyed by missiles which initiate a virus chain reaction when detonated. The real life media don't know quite what to make of this, and the novel follows a young intern reporter as she travels around Earth to meet individually in real life the refugees from a virtual planet that's been almost totally ravaged by the Primfluenza Virus. Her journey takes her from a French Chateaux to a New York apartment to a bedsit in a Hillingdon council estate. "It was terrible," one refugee – a member of the German aristocracy – tells her. "We were running around in panic because one moment everything was normal and the next it's all vapourising before our eyes. All gone, just like that. All gone. Everything." She then orders her butler to bring more tea and weeps silently for several seconds, telling our bemused protagonist, "You don't know what it's like. You don't know what it's like."

The Time Traveller's Virtual Partner. Within hours of meeting and falling in love in the metaverse, Wigander Sansom and Dostree Chan are astonished to find out that they're communicating from different time periods. Twenty-two-year-old Wigander is a full quarter-century ahead of the thirty-year-old Dostree's 2018. In 2043, it turns out, people have become nostalgic for the good old days of SL and the Ruth look is very fashionable amongst teenagers. One of many self-proclaimed 'retronauts', Wigander was spending his time exploring the thousands of abandoned regions (preserved for posterity by Google as a tax-deductible expense) when he came across 'Moonstand', a sim of space-themed fairground rides which – unbeknownst to him – runs on a server which utilises experimental memory chips made from a memristor-graphene composite. At first, the love-struck pair declare this barrier to the possibility of physical union as a meaningless triviality and rejoice in the universe finding a way to bring them together; a few days later, however, Dostree asks casually if Wigander can research 2018's winning lottery numbers for her. A month passes and Dostree becomes a millionaire many times over, but each meeting she has with Wigander sees his recollection of their previous encounters more and more degraded. Throwing caution to the wind, she buys one last winning ticket, but when she logs in to celebrate with her love, Wigander is no-where to be found. The reader is then told he was the son of the original winner of that final ticket, an unemployed writer who kept secret his fortune from his family by claiming all his money was from the sale of his Kindle novels. Without that lottery win, he doesn't feel able to ask for the hand in marriage of his girlfriend and Wigander is never born. Dostree, of course, knows none of this; just when you think it can't get any more heart-breaking, the reader is told how she looks sadly through her apartment window at the statue of 'The Railwayman', a newly erected tribute to her town's local history and the very same statue which – not a hundred pages earlier – Wigander also was noted to look at through his window. Yes, Wigander was Dostree's son.

Red Prim Rising. The Russians launch their own metaverse, Вторая жизнь созданных шахт (Second Life of Crafted Mines). Derided by western governments, it becomes an overnight internet sensation and populated by millions of disaffected Americans and Europeans. Everyone becomes friends and world peace breaks out. Well, I can dream.

42

Mesh addiction

First published January 2015, huckleberryhax.blogspot.com

About once or twice a year I become infected with the building bug and start fiddling around with prims in my skybox in Varano. Yes, you heard me: prims. Mesh might well be established now as the minimum standard in quality 3D creation in the metaverse and mesh builders might well regard the creaking inworld building system (it is, of course, powered by steam, it's so old) as something not much more sophisticated (technically, cognitively or – indeed – socially) than putting together a multicolour house with some Lego bricks; but the good old-fashioned inworld prim arrangement system has one very special virtue that appeals to me: I understand it.

It's now about eight years since my first ever SL friend, Dizi, taught me the basics of building in SL – a lesson which resulted in a rough approximation of my mother's dining room table –

and most of the items I build today would actually work perfectly withn the 2007 metaverse. Admittedly, I do have a fairly key advantage in my building projects insofar as I'm interested in recreating postwar architecture and Danish Modern furniture – or, to put it another way, I like building stuff that's naturally composed of lots of right-angles. The limitations of prim building in terms of the objects it's possible to make with them, therefore, are not often walls I knock up against.

It is, of course, quite possible to create some fairly complex objects if you combine prims cleverly and are prepared to put the time in on all the zoomed, micro-millimetre adjustments required of smoothly fitting together linksets. Unfortunately, this brings us to the other great limitation of building with prims and a wall I've found myself knocking up against all too often: the number of prims required of such work – or, to couch it in today's terms, the land impact. I currently sell a faithful reproduction of my mother's Ladderax system (yes, I admit there is a theme of sorts to my collection; it has nothing to do with unresolved childhood issues and everything to do with the availability of something I can actually measure) and it consists of 58 prims. On a standard 512 metre squared plot, that would be half your allowance gone in a single piece of furniture – and not even one you can sit or have sex on.

It's probably no great surprise to learn that I've only sold one of these so far (actually, it probably *is* a surprise to learn that I've sold even that number). This might all be about to change, however, because last week I finished creating a mesh version, and it has a land impact of just *seventeen*. Words cannot convey the sense of man-accomplishment this gives me. The mesh version looks identical to and has precisely the same amount of functionality as the original prim version: two cabinets (one for drinks with a walnut veneer, the other for storing LPs), both with opening and closing doors (and a sound effect for this sampled from the actual item), two single shelves, one shelf unit, a cupboard with opening doors and a unit with three opening and closing drawers. Even now that a few days have passed since its completion, I still look at it in awe and cannot quite escape the conclusion that I've become some sort of god.

But wait, you cry: *mesh?* Did I not mere moments ago eschew all that? I did indeed. Happily, I bought from the Marketplace last year a copy of 'Mesh Studio' by *TheBlack Box*, essentially a script you drop into the root prim (which, incidentally, is the yellow one when you've clicked edit on your object, if – like me – you spent ages wondering how people knew which prim was the root prim) of your build so that when you subsequently click on it a copy of your linkset is uploaded to a server and a download link is then sent to you in chat for a mesh conversion. Instant mesh; no messing about in *Blender* required. I adore Mesh Studio.

(A note about Mesh Snobbery: if you're not already aware of this, it still probably won't surprise you all that much to hear that *some* of the mesh builders who construct directly in *Blender* (or other comparable 3D application requiring at least an undergraduate degree in advanced geometry) express a little bit of a virtual sneer when you identify yourself as a Mesh Studio user. In fairness to them, designing in dedicated software does indeed offer infinitely more complexity than converting Lego bricks and a *Blender* skillset probably doesn't pay a great deal in hard cash, so you might as well take your recompense in superiority sneers. In fact, it's the same kind of sneer I myself use when taking slide film photographs and spot someone taking snapshots with their iPhone.)

As with all systems, there's a process to learn and tricks to understand, and issues that arise which aren't covered in the explanatory notecard and which require knowledge about mesh that's probably as obvious as the sky being blue to the experienced mesher, but which require quite a bit of trawling through web forums to get insight into if you're a complete noob to this like I am. I thought I'd gather some of the 'magic knowledge' I've acquired thus far in case you're similarly ill-equipped:

Mesh objects can only have eight 'faces', which translates as eight textures. The Mesh Studio script will alert you to how many faces you've used so far in your prim build in a bit of floaty text. Be warned: Using different colours counts as a different face, so if you've used the same texture all over your object but applied four different tints to it then that's four faces you've used.

Making unseen prim faces 100% transparent will eliminate them from the mesh build and thus reduce its eventual land impact on conversion. Choosing a transparent texture for the face will not have the same effect.

You will inevitably best learn through trial and error. Given that each time you upload a mesh object you have to pay a little, it might be best to perfect your models on the Beta Grid (where uploading is free).

Speaking of uploading, before Linden will allow you to upload mesh models to SL, you must have your payment information on file and have completed the Intellectual Property tutorial.

Once your mesh model has been imported into SL, scaling it up in size will increase its land impact. Scaling it down will usually decrease it.

When you link a mesh object to a prim, the combined land impact often goes down. For my Ladderax, I needed to link each of my cabinet doors to a cylindrical 'hinge' that contained a rotate script; the cabinet door had a land impact of 2 and the hinge a land impact of 1: when selected together they had a combined land impact of 3, but when I joined them this went down to 2. I have no idea why this works, however I assure you that I'm not complaining.

There are other mesh conversion products available, such as 'Prims to Mesh Convertor' by *egphilippov.* This product (currently L$3,000 less than Mesh Studio at an introductory price of L$1,999) offers some sort of browser-based editing of mesh objects before you import them into SL; the blurb is a little vague on what this actually enables you to do, however the reviews left so far appear to love it.

There is actually a completely free way of converting prims to mesh if you're a Firestorm user. By right-clicking on a prim object, clicking More > More > Save as > Collada, you can then save the object to your hard disk and then import it back as a mesh model. As with Mesh Studio, everything in the build must have been created by you for this to work (check scripts and textures as well as the prims themselves); a restriction to this method that does not appear to apply to Mesh Studio, however, is that individual prims with more than eight faces will break the process and cause an 'element is invalid' error on upload – so cutting a hollowed prim cube, for example, would cause this (because it creates nine faces).

Sadly, the building bug rarely lasts more than a few days in a row for me; a couple of weeks at most: the feverishness passes, the obsession over shaving off *just one more prim* passes and I emerge, slightly bleary-eyed and ready to resume life in the non-building world.

As you might have guessed, however, I'm in the midst of mesh addiction right now. I should be editing my latest novel, but I decided to write this article instead.

Afterword

Bit of an arbitrary ending? Well, the line had to be drawn somewhere. There's a future *Volume II* to start planning, after all.

The book as it stands offers glimpses into a virtual world ambling along just outside the edges of mainstream culture: well-known enough to have a reputation (an undeserved one); not well-known enough to have the sort of mass following which its architects perhaps once dreamed of. 2015, however, is going to be the year in which virtual worlds start making their way back into the public imagination.

It's already started. *Minecraft* – already a mainstream occupation for millions of youngsters – is starting to attract the somewhat bemused attention of the press. In fact, as I write this, I'm listening to a BBC radio documentary about the phenomenon. Topics covered so far have included creating virtual spaces, whole imaginary lives being led right under parents' noses and griefing in the form of the theft or destruction of virtual possessions. Any of this sound familiar? It feels slightly odd to hear such personally well-known issues discussed in relation to a completely different virtual world product. There will come a time, however, when we old-timers will nod regularly at the much-discussed virtual living news stories and tell people how a similar sort of thing used to happen in SL (and they will roll their eyes and tell us to stop droning on about ancient technology).

SL itself is starting to attract a modicum of new media interest. In place of the occasional *Whatever-happened-to-Second-Life* stories that long-term residents have been throwing their arms up in despair over for several years now, a few articles have been looking much more closely – and with interest – at the aspects of SL which have contributed to its quite astonishing longevity. The time of virtual worlds is approaching and suddenly people want to know how they work.

In my mind, that makes this the perfect moment to bring this book to a close: the pioneering era is coming to an end and anticipation is growing over what is to come. There's no guarantee, you know, that it will be better. It might just, in fact, be worse.

Call it a virtual cliff-hanger, if you will.